D0946331

Cognitive Science and Psychoanalysis

KENNETH MARK COLBY

ROBERT J. STOLLER

University of California, Los Angeles

THE ANALYTIC PRESS

1988   Hillsdale, NJ   Hove and London

The Analytic Press

Distributed solely by

Lawrence Erlbaum Associates, Inc., Publishers
365 Broadway
Hillsdale, New Jersey 07642

Library of Congress Cataloging-in-Publication Data

Colby, Kenneth Mark, 1920–
    Cognitive science and psychoanalysis / Kenneth Mark Colby and
Robert J. Stoller.
      p.   cm.
    Includes bibliographies and index.
    ISBN 0-8058-0177-4.   ISBN 0-88163-076-4 (pbk.)
    1. Psychoanalysis.   2. Cognition.   I. Stoller, Robert J.
II. Title.
[DNLM: 1. Cognition.   2. Psychoanalytic Theory.   WM 460 C686c]
    RC506.C59 1988
    616.89'17 – – dc 19
    DNLM/DLC   87-30118
    for Library of Congress   CIP

Printed in the United States of America
10 9 8 7 6 5 4 3 2 1

We thank Mrs. Flora Degen, our secretary,
for her skillful and enthusiastic assistance in this project.

Contents

v

7
OUR-SCIENCE:
THE OBSERVING-INSTRUMENT/77

8
OUR-SCIENCE:
THE TESTS ANALYSTS OFFER/93

9
FOLK PSYCHOLOGY/109

10
HOMUNCTIONALISM/123

11
HOMUNCULOSIS/123

12
COMPUTATIONAL PSYCHOLOGY/129

13
DEFLECTIONS/141

14
CONCLUSIONS/153

REFERENCES/155

INDEX/163

1
Introduction

S*: We wish, in this book, to think through some relations between two fields that are concerned with the mind—cognitive science and psychoanalysis. We intend to examine how they might be connected and contribute to one another.

To model something as complex as the mind, cognitive inquiry must use ideas of many fields, among others, psychoanalysis, because of its concern with feelings, fantasies, desires. To measure the gaps we must cross, consider our first words, "we wish." One could write a history of each discipline in which the question of aims and desire was the crucial issue forming those disciplines; yet the two histories would almost never overlap.

We are biased. We view cognitive science as a new, promising, lively field, full of novel concepts and methods about the mind, whereas psychoanalysis is and thinks of itself (at least four days of the week) as being in the doldrums. In this volume, we examine that difference in enthusiasm to show why it exists, what its effects are, and what we guess the future might hold. In regard to the theory of psychoanalysis, we take the position that it is not, as often alleged, a totally dead duck. It stands as a label for a number of ideas about mind that have a history extending indefinitely into the past and a future extending indefinitely forward, the present label "psychoanalysis" dropping away while aspects of it continue to progress. Like other fields of inquiry, the concepts and ideas of psychoanalysis will become something different: new facts and ideas will produce new

---

*When one of us has written a section, his initial will be attached; when both, both initials. But each author has edited every word and added a few of his own. In the case of impasse, the original writer wins.

theories and models that will draw from, but not be identical with, aspects of classical psychoanalysis. Many psychoanalytic ideas are fruitless and will disappear. Others will have continuing value for a cognitive science that can improve, transform, or replace psychoanalytic theses. In this regard, we shall focus on the question, dear to psychoanalysts, whether psychoanalysis is a science.

In arguing that psychoanalysis is not a science, we shall show that few scholars studying this question get to the bottom of the issue. Instead, they start by accepting, as do psychoanalytic theorists, that the reports of what happens in psychoanalytic treatment—the primary source of the data—are factual, and then they lay out their interpretations of the significance of facts for theory. We, on the other hand, question the status of the facts.

We limit the dimensions of this study. First, we leave out much of what cognitive science and psychoanalysis are about, for example, how each performs its daily work or how their inquirers deal with computational systems or psychoanalytic patients. Second, we are concerned mainly with improving ways to model the mind, a conceptual rather than an empirical task. We side with Ziman (1978), who said:

> The most sincere account that we can give of the attempt to build a science of human behavior . . . emphasizes ignorance rather than reliable knowledge. More specifically, however, to make a rational assessment of our ignorance on a particular topic—to identify enigmas and formulate consensible questions—is itself an important scientific activity. (p. 148)

Our purpose is not to discuss plans for inventing replicas of a person, such as a machine that learns, plays chess like a human, speaks, understands language, thinks, or desires. We are considering only computational models that will simulate aspects of mind sufficiently for us, by continuously improving the model, to understand more accurately how the mind works.

Grünbaum (1983, 1984), has in the last decade or more investigated the claims of psychoanalysis to be a science. He has examined these claims intensively from many angles: the pronouncements of Freud and his followers; whether psychoanalytic theories can ever be tested; whether data gathered in treatment can be used to do anything more than corroborate; the thesis (in disagreement with Popper, 1971) that some analytic ideas can be examined and refuted in the clinical situation; the efforts of experimentalists to verify psychoanalytic ideas; the hermeneuticists' reformation; errors in the logic of psychoanalytic arguments.

We believe Grünbaum's examination is more advanced, more sophisticated than psychoanalysis warrants. Grünbaum's oversight is his generosity in accepting analysts' claims that what they report as happening actually happened and only then battering the conclusions they derive therefrom. An example of his charitableness about the data is his disagreeing with Ricoeur (1974), who insists that "psychoanalysis does not satisfy the standards of the sciences of observation, and the 'facts' it deals with are not verifiable by multiple, independent observers. . . . There are no 'facts' nor any observation of 'facts' in psychoanalysis but rather the interpretation of a narrated history" (p. 186). (We, on the other hand, agree with Ricoeur, at least on this point that what is reported are "not facts.")

When Grünbaum turns to discussing the data, he says that " 'clinical data' are here construed as findings coming from *within* the psychoanalytic treatment sessions" (Laudan, 1983, p. 172). But "insofar as the credentials of psychoanalytic theory are currently held to rest on clinical findings, as most of its official spokesmen would have us believe, the dearth of acceptable and probatively cogent clinical data renders these credentials quite weak" (pp. 173-4). Our position is even more sharply negative: It is not the *dearth* of but the *impossibility* of getting inspectable observations agreed on by others that wrecks the scientific pretenses of psychoanalysis. The problem is not "that data from the couch ought to be discounted as being inadmissibly contaminated" by such effects as suggestibility (p. 175) but, even worse, that *we can never know what the data from the couch are.* Psychoanalytic evidence is hearsay, first when the patient reports his or her version of an experience and second when the analyst reports to an audience. Given that problem, the rest of Grünbaum's arguments for and against psychoanalysis as science are premature if not superfluous.

Farrell (1981), on the other hand, is constantly alert to the flaw in "the material of the case." For instance, regarding Freud, he says, "No notes are, or ever could be, anything like a *full* account of what happened. Reference to [his] posthumously published notes shows us that . . . they were to a large extent abstracts from and summaries of what happened" (p. 58). Or, "The impact which a patient makes on [an analyst] is typically so great and so immediate that it strikes him as absurd and downright ignorant to suggest that, in his reports, he is 'doctoring' or 'filtering' or 'reconstructing' what the patient is giving him" (p. 60). Or, "The [case] material is artefact-infected" (p. 129). (And we join those not thrilled by psychoanalysts' claims that each psychoanalytic treatment is an experiment, as that word is used in science. We find it honorable enough—no mean contribution to knowledge—that a psychoanalysis can be an exploration, an intense observation of a unique human creature.)

We can only agree with Wallerstein (1986) that Ricoeur's " 'confirmatory constellation,' i.e. the criteria of coherence, of inner consistency, and of narrative intelligibility" (p. 421) can hardly a science make. However, Wallerstein, in his papers on psychoanalysis as science, does not use our criterion of reliable data as a sine qua non of science. Though we believe the vignettes that make up psychoanalytic case reports are myths and metaphors that may contain powerful truths, he is optimistic "that there is sufficient warrant" to believe that with their data analysts can be "loyal to the canons of objective scientific method" (p. 446). We prefer Peterfreund's (1986) position: "I believe that if psychoanalysis is to be taken as a serious science and if its conclusions or findings are to be assigned any truth value, its practitioners will have to stop reporting without supporting evidence and without specifying the nature of the process that generated the findings claimed" (p. 132).

Let us say I experience a patient's affect as intense. (And, for this example, let us put aside the problem that, were you there, you might interpret that affect not as "intense" but as "forced" or "histrionic" or as a substitute for another—hidden—affect.) Now, writing about it, I choose not "intense," but "primitive" or "narcissistic". Can you see how, out of your reach, I have shifted a clinical description to one that aims toward theory proving? Or insult concealed by scientific vocabulary? ("Homosexuals suffer from primitive affects such as narcissistic rage, which makes them borderline personalities.")

Colby and I believe a whole other system of inquiry and testing is needed. Science is composed of many parts and processes that by themselves are not science. A hunch is not a science, nor is a guess, nor is an interpretation, nor is a reconstruction, nor even is a clue. A theory is not a science, nor are several theories, nor even a system of theories. A hypothesis is not a science, nor is a series of hypotheses. A model or constellation of models is not a science. Even when you link all those into one construction—"an explanatory edifice"—you do not have a science, though each is a part of science. For without the final ingredient—dependable, manipulable, shared data—you still may end up with a religion, an ethical system, one of the humanities, art criticism, a *Weltanschauung,* or a practice, such as astrology or alchemy. Psychoanalysis fails in the task of modeling the mind scientifically and has always failed since Freud wrote his first words. Our suggestion is that a scientific theory of mental activity lies instead in the direction of cognitive science.

We know how long it can take for an idea to have its effect. Here is Nagel in 1959 speaking to the deaf ears of psychoanalysts:

> Although in the interview the analyst is supposedly a "passive" auditor of the "free association" narration by the subject, in point of fact the analyst does direct the course of the narrative. This by itself does not necessarily impair the evidential worth of the outcome, for even in the most meticulously conducted laboratory experiment the experimenter intervenes to obtain the data he is after. There is nevertheless the difficulty that in the nature of the case the full extent of the analyst's intervention is not a matter that is open to public scrutiny, so that by and large one has only his own testimony as to what transpires in the consulting room. It is perhaps unnecessary to say that this is not a question about the personal integrity of psychoanalytic practitioners. The point is the fundamental one that no matter how firmly we may resolve to make explicit our biases, no human being is aware of all of them, and that objectivity in science is achieved through the criticism of publicly accessible material by a community of independent inquirers. . . . Moreover, unless data are obtained under carefully standardized circumstances, or under different circumstances whose dependence on known variables is nevertheless established, even an extensive collection of data is an unreliable basis for inference. To be sure, analysts apparently do attempt to institute standard conditions for the conduct of interviews. But there is not much information available on the extent to which the standardization is actually enforced, or whether it relates to more than what may be superficial matters. (pp. 49-50)

C: Cognitive science is the systematic inquiry into aspects of the human mind amenable to explanation by way of a computational analogy. William James (1890) took psychology to be the science of mental activity. In the first volume of his *Principles*, he opened with:

> Psychology is the Science of Mental Life, both of its phenomena and their conditions. The phenomena are such things as we call feelings, desires, cognitions, reasonings, decisions and the like: and, superficially considered, their variety and complexity is such as to leave a chaotic impression on the observer.

Almost 100 years later, we still do not have a science of these phenomena. Psychoanalysis was a good try that failed, and behaviorism, suffering a mindless blindness to, and evasion of, the phenomena in question, did not try at all. Cognitive science contributes to a scientific psychology through the construction of computational models whose processes are assumed to be analogous to those unknown mental processes that produce and direct human behavior. The models satisfy a theory of the patterns or regularities of the phenomena. A theory is a system of concepts and hypotheses specifying the design of an ideal system intended to apply to real empirical systems.

The concepts and hypotheses of the theory stem from many sources, including the folk psychology used to describe the phenomena in everyday language terms. Another source is the two-millenia philosophy of mind, some of which Freud rewrote as psychoanalysis and tried to apply to clinical problems. Our position is that some "psychoanalytic" ideas are still live, programmable options for cognitive science, especially in instances of extreme deflection from the ideal mental system that come to the attention of the clinician.

S: It is the responsibility of writers to help their readers, either with explicit instructions or by indirection, to know how to read them. Let me therefore describe problems inherent in our making this book, in the hope that once manifest they will improve our chances of being understood.

Colby and I are different in personality. He has a scientist's mind; I do not. I enjoy the clinical, especially practicing psychoanalysis as treatment; he has long since moved from there. He writes in a clear, impersonal, scientific style; I try to make my writing seem as if I were talking. I enjoy being unendingly immersed in psychoanalysis and even thrive on despairing of it. Colby attacks problems directly and pries them open with logic and vast knowledge, confident that in time the apparent muddle of mind-at-work will be transformed into specifiable rules; I think that, in time, he and those like him will do so but that I am not one of them: Colby loves chess and plays it well; I never even learned the rules.

So it is odd when two different types nonetheless find themselves in agreement. And when it comes time to write down our agreements—no more just sitting in the office and yelling enthusiastically at each other—problems in writing styles arise that must be resolved and at the same time not hidden, since the differences in style reflect differences in approach, content, and the weighing of significance. Can the two of us, then, maintain our individuality—it is part of the content of what we say—and not leave readers confused?

Our second big problem in the writing is our audience. If we write for cognitive scientists, then we each must pick a style and language that honors *that* audience; if we are talking primarily to psychoanalysts, we must speak in a different way. Yet both styles must convey the same main ideas. If we want to aim at both audiences, still other techniques of writing must be used. If we imagine there are others out there who deserve our concern—philosophers of science, psychologists, astrophysicists, chefs, bookbinders—then still other problems in writing must be solved. And the solutions are required at every moment, in the choice of each word and in the form of each sentence. With two such different people as Colby and me, and with even a minimum of two such different audiences as cognitive scientists and psychoanalysts, we certainly have our problems. So we use these few words now to keep our audience from being jarred by our disparities.

A final orientation. We make our choices on how and what to write with the idea that most of our readers will be cognitive scientists, philosophers of science, their students, and informed laymen.

We begin first with our views of what current cognitive inquiry is about and then fill out the above-mentioned claims about interfield relations between cognitive science and psychoanalysis.

2

Science and Cognitive Inquiry

Knowledge is that part of ignorance that we arrange and classify.

—A. Bierce

Science has a firm determination not to persist in error if any exertion of hand or mind can deliver us from it.

—Medawar

C': If we take the stand that psychoanalysis is not a science, we might then reasonably be asked, What *is* science? It is not so easy these days to say what science is.

Consider a few one-sentence textbook descriptions and prescriptions—Science is the systematic and rational study of nature. The aim of scientific inquiry is to solve problems set by scientific fields using scientific methods and principles of rationality. Scientific inquiry uses theories, observations, experiments, and measurements to arrive at and extend reliable knowledge about the world. Scientists deduce empirical consequences from hypotheses, and if such consequences are true, the hypotheses are accepted as true. Science involves metaphysics, theories, data, aims, and methods, all of which evolve over time.

More slogans. Science runs on consensibility (agreement about meanings of terms) and consensus regarding truth (Ziman, 1978). Science seeks to make true statements about the universe. Scientific knowledge accumulates and arrives at ever-closer approximations to reality. Scientific inquiry produces public records of information and opinion that are open to inspection, scrutiny, and criticism by others.

9

Science provides an opportunity for the methods of inquiry to be reproduced by others who obtain roughly the same results. Science explains patterns of observation by describing patterns of imperceptible entities. Science strives for impersonal, objective, reproducible knowledge about the world.

Further textbook canons: Scientific observation relies on intersubjective agreements of experts' pattern-recognition judgments, which in part are their theories of the objects in question. Science combines concepts, mathematics, and, observations to yield epistemically and pragmatically useful knowledge. Science has norms and standards of logical consistency, verifiability, and falsifiability. Scientific inquiry attempts to eliminate errors by falsifying conjectured hypotheses. Science as systematic inquiry generates taxonomic and explanatory knowledge in an attempt to understand factual and conceptual objects. Science tries to understand what is possible and what is not possible in the world. Science searches for laws, precise descriptions of regularities. Science is governed by an ethics or morality regarding acquiring, communicating, disseminating, and using scientific knowledge.

Final maxims: Through feedback control, systematic, rational, scientific inquiry self-corrects errors and omissions. Scientific knowledge is methodical, fallible, self-critical, partial, and defeasible. Science explains by fitting an event into a discernible pattern. The aim of science is to solve conceptual and empirical problems by answering why or how-does-it-work questions. Scientific activity is perpetual problem solving, continuously facing new situations and new problems. In its natural history phase, scientists observe, describe, and classify; in its theoretical phase, scientists formulate theories with deducible empirical consequences.

> *Ask a scientist what he conceives the scientific method to be, and he will adopt an expression that is at once solemn and shifty-eyed.*
>
> —Medawar, 1969

Adding further canons or prescriptions to the above would not be much more illuminating. One cannot define science (or anything else) by a set of necessary and sufficient conditions. No activities are performed by all—and only—scientists. It being a matter of decision more than definition, the best we can do is stipulate features of a cluster-concept that might allow inquiry to be recognized as scientific. As nonphilosophers of science, we may be presumptuous to go this far, but we do.

Science is *about* something called the world, the universe, reality. Immediately we plunge into metaphysics, ways of looking at this reality. For no unique "real" can be found; there are several realities and several ways of describing them.

> *It is venturesome to suggest that a co-ordination of words*
> *can resemble the universe very much.*

> —Borges

At bottom, we assume a deep structure of the universe, R_o (the GROK), ineffable, undescribable, unpicturable, and about which we know nothing. We further assume that R_o generates a manifest structure, the objects making up R_1. Aspects of R_1-objects are experienced by human sensory channels as R_2-objects. R_2 objects that we take as interest relative and significant we interpret as R_3. We abstract from the directly and indirectly perceivable manifestations of R_2 by pruning information from R_2, discarding it as negligible. What we take as concrete particulars are the conjoint products of a combination of recursive abstraction operations (algorithms) that constitute the human mind. The resultant R_3 objects are superimpositions of rules of conceptual categories, digitized (categorized) from the analog information received from R_2. Systematic critical/scientific inquiry is directed at R_2-R_3 relations.

> *What we observe is not nature itself but nature exposed*
> *to our method of questioning.*

> —Heisenberg

One more slogan: Science aims for explanatory theoretical knowledge, a systematic R_3, effective in solving problems in the R_2-R_3 domain. (The cognitive inquirer then faces a complication in that he takes the R_3 of "construers"—people using knowledge to achieve their goals—as his R_2.) Theories, constructed by human imagination, are called on to solve problems in R_2-R_3. Theories specify the schematic design of an idealized system that is compared to aspects of empirical systems of the intended reference class. (Theories and models are discussed further in chapter 12). Described observations on empirical systems contribute to evaluating theories. As we discuss, psychoanalytic theories have lacked adequate evaluation not because the "data" are unsupportive but simply because no reliable data exist to begin with. This does not mean there are no observable events or phenomena to be described. To become scientific data, the raw information (say, a tape recording of utterances) must first be preprocessed by converting it to a written transcript. Next, relevant segments or units of the transcript must be selected. Finally, the information in the segments must be encoded into the categories and terminology of the theory. Our claim is that the reports offered in the psychoanalytic literature are renditions too unfaithful to qualify as scientific data since they are mainly fictives and factoids.

The natural sciences are devoted to nature, the human sciences to man. But man is a part of nature, not apart from nature. Man in nature is like a tree in the ground, not like a pebble in a box. The division "Natural sciences versus artifactual sciences" is helpful only if we ignore that nothing in nature measures itself. In this sense, all science is artifactual: the happenings of physics, for instance, are produced in part by physicists themselves. A manmade object, like a computing system, is indirectly a part of nature, but few people allow that computer science or artificial intelligence are natural sciences. Artificial intelligence is a mixture of science and technology, providing theories and models of our minds and developing techniques for constructing physicosymbolic simulations of ourselves, thus contributing to an opportunity for experimental epistemology. These efforts contribute a computational theory of mind to cognitive science. Our position is that cognitive science, a human nature science, is a natural science even though the human mental system has a large artifactual component, namely its semantic representations.

Another favorite dichotomy is "general versus special sciences." Physics is general because all objects are physical (token physicalism). Special sciences take this for granted and add further specializing taxonomies, such as "living," "semantic," and the like. The unity of science (if we mean more than token physicalism) is a myth we should outgrow. A skim through an issue of *Current Contents* shows that science is ever more diverse and pluralistic, evolving and diverging in many directions, each domain having a specialized vocabulary, concepts, methods, and instruments.

Science as critical inquiry evolves over time, generating new phenomena and new interests. Theories, data, methods, aims, and their metaphysics change. The traditional aim of knowledge for knowledge's sake has been enlarged by the quest for *valuable* knowledge that helps humans get what they consider to be of positive value and to avoid, reduce, be freed of, or prevent what is disvalued. Cognitive comfort and pragmatic comfort have been continuous aims in the growth of scientific knowledge. The value of satisfying human curiosity (regarding black holes or the age of the universe, for example) exists alongside the strong push toward knowledge that leads to changing the world through a praxis.

In current prescriptions for science we would include a greater concern for using resources to solve problems that matter in human living, rather than leaving it to a chance fallout from other sciences. Effective sciences lead to a technology that has high likelihood of success. Computer technology has made it possible to be clearer about highly complicated processes and to create new objects that aid human understanding and praxis.

Computational psychology, growing out of artificial intelligence, advances the human sciences by providing a new, systematic, praxis-oriented inquiry procedure: idealizing computational model construction. Computational models of complex mental processes embody idealized, theoretical, explanatory knowledge of value not just in understanding, but in guiding action to modify processes that produce human suffering and misery arising from the problems of psychosocial living.

Psychiatry is concerned with the diagnosis and treatment of mental illness, but it has been unable to define mental health or mental illness or to create a reliable classification scheme of its "illnesses" (Colby and Spar, 1983). The hospital psychiatrist observes conditions that may deserve the label"mental disorder." But most patients seen in office practice suffer from the dilemmas and buffettings of inter-personal life. The problems of those patients require greater under-standing of the mind at the semantic-structure, personal-construal level as well as the development of expert systems, technologic semantic interventions effective at the level of cognitive penetrability. For the relief of mental suffering, we need a computer-based psychoeducational technology to help people choose wiser bases of actions in stress-producing situations. Such computer programs, like expert systems in artificial intelligence, can provide a new systematic procedure for guiding valued psychologic change (Colby, 1986).

A 19th-century distinction between the natural sciences *(Naturwissenschaften)* and mental sciences *(Geisteswissenschaften)* has resurfaced in hermeneutics. It deals with interpretations of meanings of "texts," including spoken communications. Hermeneutics claims that natural science does not provide knowledge of people and societies, because it does not take into account the centrality of communicative action and discourse involving interpretations of meanings implicit in natural language and social institutions. We agree that attempts to solve problems of classes of people's minds must generalize and explain at the semantic level, where representa-tional content consists of personal construals (to construe is to invest with meaning) codified in symbols (Abelson, 1981). The hermeneutic "sciences" have a like domain of objects—people using a language—

but their problem-solving effectiveness is thus far undemonstrated. The doubts about hermeneutics in systematic inquiry is not that human behavior as a system of signs cannot be "read" as a "text" and interpreted. Rather, we simply cannot find therein the procedures for deciding *which* interpretation of *what* has explanatory usefulness and is more accurate, fruitful, or effective than another for solving human-world problems.

Systematic inquiry that leads to a science of mental systems and processes takes personal construals as its empirical domain. A person as an active symboling agent with a goal-pursuing mental system contains and uses his construed knowledge to reach goals through informed actions. A rock is not an active symboling goal-pursuing system capable of forming construals of its experience. Since it is a mere aggregate, or heap, it contains information$_1$, (analog information of stimulus patterns [Dretske, 1981]), but it is not a system that digitizes information$_1$ into information$_2$ (construals) nor does it try to use information$_2$ to achieve goals. A book contains information$_2$ organized by its author but is not an active agent using it to achieve goals. A person constructs knowledge and appropriately uses it to achieve goals and satisfy interests. Computing systems, people and cells are construing goal-pursuing systems with interests; rocks and books are not.

A developed cognitive science as human nature science, working toward a scientific theory of the mind, will draw on information from artificial intelligence, psychology (folk, psychoanalytic, cognitive), philosophy, linguistics, and neuroscience (Colby, 1978). Although psychoanalytic theory has been scientifically ineffective, we emphasize herein the possible relations between an emerging cognitive science and those psychoanalytic concepts that may not yet have run out of vitality, particularly in the area of extremely deflected mental processes characterized by purposive *mis*construals.

3
Preliminaries

> *First, the taking in of scattered particulars under one Idea*, so that everyone understands what is being talked about. . . . *Second, the separation of the Idea into parts, by dividing it at the joints, as nature directs, not breaking any limb in half as a bad carver might.*

> —Plato, *Phaedrus* 265C (italics added).

C: In these pages we repeatedly use an analogy (stronger than metaphor) between poorly understood human mental systems and better understood computing systems. The analogy involves an equivalence assumption. Consider Figure 1, which portrays an equivalence between two systems, computing and mental. The computing systems we are familiar with are modern computers, whose components can be divided into hardware, instruction set, and programs. The instruction set (the programmer's manual) that comes with the hardware makes it possible for programs to be constructed in programming languages and run on the hardware device.

We assume the human mental (hereafter mental) system has an innate, species-specific, capacity for symbol-processing, a basic software resource (e.g. the capacity to acquire natural language) that comes with the wetware of our neural system. Supervenient on these two biologic levels is a semantic level, termed the "intentional" in philosophical psychology. (For further discussion of these levels see Pylyshyn, 1984, as well as Newell, 1982.) The semantic level (representations of beliefs, goals, affects, etc.) shall concern us in this book. We have nothing to say about lower biologic levels or models of neural connectionism. We assume neural-level presence as necessary

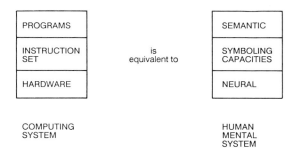

Figure 1. Equivalence of Computing Systems and Mental Systems.

for realizing semantic content. The semantic structure-types of symbol-expressions, encoded personal construals, assign meanings to the incoming tokens and exert control by means of distinctive semantic content. The physicochemical embodiment at the neural level allows the semantic structure-types to coproduce behavior. Construals have causal powers in virtue of their physical instantiation. Physical embodiment of a program helps heal the Cartesian cut by allowing thing systems (res extensa) to become thinking systems (res cogitans) whose productions are simultaneously the result of neural processes under physicochemical laws and the result of derivations under meaning-preserving computational rules that eventuate in message controls to effectors.

> Intelligent systems are what they are from being ground between the nether millstone of their physiology or hardware, which sets inner limits on their adaptation, and the upper millstone of a complex, environment, which places demands on them for change. (Simon, 1981).

Our initial analogy asserts that mental systems and modern computer systems are instances of computational systems that take in, manipulate, transform, and produce symbolic expressions. We shall not debate whether the analogy is justified. (All analogies limp, and when pushed the disanalogies eventually become too great.)

Provisional adoption of an analogy expands the properties that can be studied in the recipient (mental) system as properties are transferred from the donor (computing) system. When Harvey proposed that the blood was circulated by the heart acting as a pump, the analogy made circulation accessible to study in terms of such properties as volumes, flow, speed, and the like. Similarly, the computational analogy, rich in consequences, opens up many questions as we hypothesize that the unknown system has (or, by disanalogy, does not have) properties of the known system. We would apply this computational perspective to only some aspects of the mind, using it until it fails, whereupon other analogies must be imagined. The question is not whether the mind "is" a computational system, but whether it can be adequately modeled by a computational system.

> *The heart of all major discoveries in the physical sciences is the discovery of novel methods of representation and so of fresh techniques by which inferences can be drawn— and drawn in ways which fit the phenomena under investigation.*
>
> —S. Toulmin (1957, p. 34)

In carving out (as Plato recommended) a semantic level of representations (construals, significations, meanings) that conform to explanatory principles different from biologic principles, one raises the issue of the autonomy of psychology (see p. 21). The semantic level is characterized by codified content (personal construals) whose origin lies in a person's historical informational transactions with his environment (whose most salient and goal-relevant aspects are other people) and with himself. The codified construals constitute meanings deriving from experienced covariation with an external and an internal world in which symbol-expressions are constructed to allow access to other symbol-expressions. The construals direct actions that have advantageous outcomes for a person in that his sought-after goals are satisfied. The properties of objects and events, having places in the patterns of the causal structure of external and internal worlds, have covariant places in the codified patterns of symbol expressions. For example, the role of the construals in psychologic implicational relations encodes the role of the properties experienced in the cause–effect relations of the internal and external worlds. Present circumstances activate relevant codifications (effective construals of past experience) because they are recognized as similar to those past circumstances in which a desired outcome was or was not obtained. In communicative action, the activated codifications produce observable patterns of objects such as linguistic expressions that vehicle the construals of underlying semantic content.

Inserting this principled type-token level between commonsense psychology and neuroscience provides relief from an absolutist eliminative materialism that insists, because of the weaknesses of folk psychology, that mental systems must be explained entirely in biologic terms. Improving on folk psychology need not wait for neuroscience. The belief that the concepts of folk psychology will be completely replaced by neural concepts is itself a folk belief. Higher-level descriptions of subjective experience will always be necessary to characterize the gross mental phenomena constituting the explananda. The underlying explanatory mechanisms will be couched in the language of a computational theory of mind.

The equivalence relation depicted in Figure 1 is elaborated in chapter 12. For now, let us simply mention that equivalence here means similarity of structure between computing programs and semantic levels. Since similarity comes in degrees, there can be weak, rough, and strong equivalences. Also, "semantic structures" here do not refer to material structure but to symbolic-expressions (construals) with physical groundings, allowing them to become physically executable and thus having causal powers. The formality condition requiring symbol-tokens to be distinguishable because of different physical shapes (Fodor, 1980) is only a realization constraint necessary for physical execution. It provides no restrictions on the semantic construals (meaningfulness) assigned to the tokens.

> In physics, symbols represent physical magnitudes and the relations among them; they are a notation for the subject matter only. . . . In cognitive science, as in computing, symbols not only refer to some extrinsic domain (say, numbers or beliefs) but they are also real objects in their own right that the machine (or, by hypothesis, the mind) manipulates in a manner that preserves the semantic properties of those symbols.
>
> —Pylyshyn, 1983

METAPHORS, ANALOGIES, ALGORITHMS

> *An algorithm is a precise instruction which determines a computational process that leads from variable initial data to the result sought for.*
>
> —Markov

> *. . . sick with desire*
> *And fastened to a dying animal*
> *It knows not what it is.*
>
> —Yeats

Yeats is speaking of the mind. We could shrug off an assumed equivalence between computing systems and mental systems with

"It's just a metaphor." The mere-metaphor dismissor considers the equivalence to be ornamental, not scientific. But metaphors express a similarity (resemblance of relations) that can be so strengthened in science as to be taken as "true."

Metaphoric expressions are abbreviated, suppressed, or ellipted similes that draw comparisons between two systems from two domains or fields. "X is like Y" and "X is adequately modeled by Y" eventually may become "X is a Y". (The heart is like a pump . . . the heart is adequately modeled by a pump . . . the heart is a pump). Features of the primary system X (the recipient) are seen in terms of features of a secondary system Y (the donor) (Black, 1979). Theory construction makes this epistemic move when the recipient system of one domain, with objects X, is poorly understood and the donor system from another domain, with objects Y, is better understood in that we know more about how its objects work to produce the phenomena in question. The hope is to increase understanding of how the recipient system works by projecting or transferring properties from the donor system so that the two come to share properties.

Classical examples (successful ones—lots of metaphors failed) involved comparison of the heart to a pump, the body to a clock, an atom to a solar system, natural selection to artificial selection, light waves to water waves, electricity to a fluid flow. The properties can be manifest features or abstract relations, and the donor system may itself be described as metaphor in another domain. The similarities drawn offer a fresh view of unsolved conceptual problems and animate new kinds of searches, particularly when donor systems offer new artifacts such as radar for bat echolations, power steering for voluntary muscle control, and computing systems for mental systems.

A conceptual problem for theories of mind (sometimes called "Brentano's problem" [Pylyshyn, 1984, p. 26] has long been how the mental, taken as nonphysical, symbolic, and semantic in nature, could explain the behavior of a physical system such as a person. How can ethereal and nonspatiotemporal "meanings" (intentional states) have causal effects on spatiotemporal systems? The conceptual obstacle posed by this mysterious relation has been demystified by the analogy with a computing system, in which symbolic representations are embodied in physical instantiations at the hardware level where the causal laws of physics and chemistry operate. It is this ostensible and apodictic demonstration that represents a great step forward in psychology and philosophy. It is a breakthrough because it breaks the back of Brentano's problem. In mental systems, the semantic level is embodied in the biologic levels in the encoded construals, the embodiments being equivalence classes of physical properties. Because they are embodied, the meanings take up space and time and thereby can have causal effects on certain spatio-temporal systems.

Introduction of new features from the donor system expands conceptual possibilities, provides new horizons to explore and new inferences to be drawn, and can lead to a reconceptualization of the recipient domain's subject matter. (For example, the computational theory and model of PARRY (Colby, 1981) reconceptualizes paranoidness, changing it from being viewed as a disease to being viewed a mode of processing symbolic expressions under a specific kind of distress.) An analogy using multiple properties is stronger than a simple, one-property metaphor. The properties selected are considered important for the domain, and thus the selection is a value-dependent operation. As more properties of the donor system transfer into the recipient system, the descriptive vocabulary becomes like that of the donor, and the metaphoric quality fades.

When the analogy is close (the model is deemed adequate because it fits well), literal expressions replace metaphors and are guides to new actions that would not be undertaken otherwise. Metaphors are appropriate or not, whereas literal expressions are effective or not. The computational analogy is more than an as-if metaphoric redescription of the phenomena; the inserted type-token semantic level is embodied in a physiology where cause-effect relations of physics connect this level to the input-output phenomena. Pylyshyn (1984) maintains that computation is a literal model of mental activity, because the model generates behavior in essentially the same way, by virtue of the same functional mechanisms and by virtue of having the same semantic content (p. 43).

A homology is a sameness or similarity of relation. In biology, morphologic structures (such as the wings of a bird and the forelimbs of land mammals) are considered homologous when they are similar in the pattern of their components and have a common ancestry in evolutionary descent. The wings of a bird and the wings of a butterfly are analogous in function but not homologous in anatomical structure of common descent. A functional homology, not limited to anatomical structures, involves a sameness or similarity of functions fulfilled in (roughly) the same way. A higher level function in members of an equivalence class is decomposable into some (not necessarily all) similar shared subfunctions.

At the semantic level, the computational analogy represents a functional homology that assumes shared abstract invariants (computational functions, algorithms) that produce the shared empirical invariants. Members of an empirical resemblance class share the manifest properties defining the class. To account for the regularities of this sharing, in-common abstract properties are hypothesized in the form of underlying algorithms composed of functions and subfunctions producing the cluster of manifest properties. The shared algorithms of resemblance classes constitute more than a purely formal analogy because a construed semantic content must be shared as well. The sameness of semantic content is functionally responsible for producing sameness in manifest input/output patterns and for differences in semantic content in these manifest patterns. The samenesses and differences in semantic content (made explicit in a programmed model) are represented formally (syntactically) in symbolic expressions such that the relevant token distinctions can be made at the physical level to produce distinct behaviors. Sharing executable algorithms implies that the same jobs—types of productive processes—are being done with differences lying only at the token level. For example, "I," "ich," "yo," "io," and "je" have token (physical shape) differences but perform the same job (fulfill the same function) as first person singular pronouns in their respective languages.

A triple analogy (pattern similarity) is involved here. First, algorithmic processes are postulated to simulate (be similar to) the unknown real processes. Second, the postulated algorithmic processes are considered to be functionally homologous to computational processes whose causal and control processes are known to exist. Third, both processes—postulated and known-to-exist—produce similar effects, that is, patterns of tokens of types characteristic of the natural kinds involved.

AUTONOMOUS PSYCHOLOGY

Two issues are involved in the claim that psychology should be an autonomous field. One asserts that psychology, a special science studying mental processes, is autonomous in the sense of conducting a systematic pursuit independent of physics, biology, and even neuroscience. The second claim is that mental processes can be studied independent of the environment's contributions.

The first issue can be considered in the light of Figure 1, in which a semantic level is portrayed as distinct from (having its own properties and regularities), *but not detached* from, the functional architecture (Pylyshyn, 1984) made up of the symboling capacity and

neural levels. Regularities and organizational principles at the semantic level cannot be captured by neural or physico-chemical generalizations, since these fields have no reductive counterparts to symbolic
entities. Nor do they offer constraints on semantic contents or
operations. Deploying the computational analogy, different computers, and different programs running on the same computer, can
execute the same algorithm, a specified process-type for getting a
desired result. The same algorithm has the same semantic content
and performs the same job-role. Descriptions of the algorithm are first
cast informally in the vocabulary of computationalese, a mentalese
characteristic of computational psychology, and then more formally
in a programming language. Computational modelers, whose beliefs
are settled enough to proceed this way, agree on this point.

Again, and with emphasis, the semantic level (Fig. 1) is distinct
from, but not detached from, the neural level. Neuroscience will not
replace cognitive science any more than hardware descriptions can
replace program descriptions. The relation between the fields is
part-whole computational and dependent on how the parts and
processes are delineated and enumerated. (Bechtel, 1983). A part-
whole composition relation is not an identity relation. A hardware
description of what is happening in a running computer system at the
level of device parts, such as on-off switches, would yield accurate
but massively stupefying details of little use in answering questions
about distinctive semantic content or about what the overall system
can be interpreted as "doing." Meaningfulness (aboutness) is an
unremovable property of a program. Even at the lowest
hardware/device level the configurations of switches of a running
program is *about* something. Theory-reduction, in the classic sense of
complete theory-replacement, is a well-worn myth in science
(Wimsatt, 1972, 1980).

More controversial than the neuroscience issue is the claim of
psychology's independence from causal or lawlike organism-
environment relations with the "natural" environment. (For most
people, the "natural" found-in-nature is predominantly artificial.)

Methodological solipsism (a mouthful first offered by Russell and
then taken up by Carnap, Putnam, and Fodor) asserts the impossibility of a naturalistic psychology linking semantic properties of
representations (truth and reference) to an external world (Fodor,
1980). It claims that until we have a complete scientific description
with the ultimate "correct" categories of the objects of the environment, we cannot have exceptionless laws relating these objects to the
representations. This claim seems overly restrictive for two reasons.
First, to explain how a mental system works, we do not need strict,

exceptionless laws. We can satisfy predictive and explanatory goals using regularities and rules of reference classes, with known exceptions being treated as special cases. These regularities and rules consist of default assumptions about what is typical and what holds in the absence of countervailing conditions (Minsky, 1986; Holland, Holyoak, Nisbett & Thagard, 1986). (In tennis and chess, if your opponent does not show up or is unable to provide opposition, you win by default.) Default rules are immune to counterexamples until the exceptions become so numerous as to override the rules. When expectations based on rules about what is typical are fulfilled, that is, an expected type is instantiated, the rules are winners (Nelson, 1982, p. 187). If expectations are disrupted, a nonwinning rule may still be useful since it is easily modified by further information allowing for special cases. (Cats have tails, except for Manx cats.) Rules allow a range of actions (action-types), leaving room for the play and novelty so characteristic of human behavior. The drawback of rule-based default assumptions with numerous implicit or explicit provisos (large *ceteris paribus* clauses to accommodate exceptions) is that if they are overvalued or accepted too rigidly, the system is in for a lot of surprises, many of them unpleasant.

A second objection to the requirement of exceptionless laws with the ultimate correct categories is that regularities with default assumptions need involve only mundane features of objects goal relevant, salient to, and typical of the construers of a resemblance class who use a shared commonsense taxonomy, not a "scientific" taxonomy. Such properties as truth and reference to an external world are not intrinsic to the content of the construed representations themselves but require second-order evaluations of the success of actions guided by these construals. The mind itself considers from *its* perspective that, say, a belief is correct (of worth) if it contributes to the satisfaction of expected goals. Increasing the value of a parameter (e.g., a credence-value) associated with the construed content strengthens such a serviceable belief. To an observer, the belief might be considered incorrect because it is not "true" according to his knowledge (i.e., his construal) of organism-environment relations.

Unless one assumes specific, innate semantic *content* (not just constraints or mechanisms), the encoded construals of the semantic level individuate commonsense kinds and explain sequences of events that the kinds participate in. They derive from, and covary with, cause–effect relations with objects of the life experience of the organism. (Plato believed our innate content came from the soul's empirical experience in an earlier life.) The content of psychologic inference rules is an example. In the rule "If X is a Y, then X has A or

X does B," the psychosemantic content of X, Y, A and B determines their connection, which may be temporal, causal, entailing, or plain nonnecessitative associative, "goes-with." The sequences of code tokenings in the construals covary with the cause–effect sequences in the environment consistently (faithfully) enough that expected goals are satisfied. The tokenings successively interact in ways consistent with what they mean, that is, their interpretation. The symbolic expressions of the code-tokenings preserve the commonsense kinds and the cause–effect relations they represent.

More vivid examples are found in the extreme deflections (departures from the theoretical ideal) like paranoia (Colby, 1975) and the "perversions" (Stoller, 1975b). In these conditions, the history-dependent provenance of semantic content must play a part in explaining such deflections. Explanations can answer questions both about how a system works and about how it got to be the way it is. For example, the theory underlying the computational model PARRY (Colby, 1981) explains how the paranoid system reacts to input patterns construed as malevolently intended. The theory asserts nothing about how the system came to be differentially sensitive to particular input patterns such that, in the particular case of PARRY, a reference to its education activates shame but a reference to its geographic origin does not. In constructing PARRY we assumed that in the maturation of mental systems, certain topic areas (free parameters) become shameful as a result of learning and teaching. Each culture socializes its members to be ashamed of some things but not others. If one is to understand why a person is ashamed of, for example, his educational status, one must know his history in relation to this topic. If his personal construal is cognitively penetrable and information-sensitive, his representations can be reconstrued to varying extent by semantic-cognitive interventions designed to alter psychologic rules and beliefs deriving from childhood. These interventions may involve challenging the historical source of the rules and their inappropriateness for solving problems in the complications and dilemmas that produce the sufferings of adult interpersonal life.

For the cognitive interventionist, it is not the "truth" of the construed rules that is at stake. It is whether the rules of a person's construed world are appropriately effective in solving misery-producing problems and dilemmas of the human world. "Don't cross the street by yourself" may be a good rule for a child, but it is outdated for an adult. Revising and conditionalizing the rigid command rules of childhood reference frames plays a large part in therapeutic learning programs (Colby, Gould, Aronson, & Colby, 1987).

4

Merits and Shortcomings
of Psychoanalysis

I feel sure that a good deal of his [Freud] more theoretical expositions were, as he would certainly have agreed, responses to his own intellectual needs rather than assertions of general validity.

—Ernest Jones

A science which hesitates to forget its founders is lost.

—Whitehead

C: Assume, for the usual sake of argument, that a field of systematic inquiry consists of (a) a community of active inquirers embedded in a host society; (b) a domain of objects for discourse in a special vocabulary; (c) metaphysical theses regarding the nature of the domain objects; (d) a stock of theories, models, concepts, hypotheses, generalizations, and data relevant to the domain; (e) a set of problems to be solved; (f) a set of aims of active inquirers trying to solve the problems of the domain and to improve its knowledge; (g) a set of methods for solving problems by scrutable theoretical and empirical procedures; and (h) an ethos of intellectual honesty, integrity, skepticism, and freedom to pursue inquiry.

A mature science approximates all these criteria, a protoscience only some. A pseudoscience advertises itself as possessing these properties even though it does not. Protoscience is different in degree; pseudoscience is different in kind (Bunge, 1983). A vast and bitterly contested literature on the topic leaves the status of psychoanalysis uncertain as a natural or special science (see, for example, Edelson, 1977; Farrell, 1981; Grünbaum, 1984; Nagel, 1959; Popper,

1971; Rubinstein, 1980). Instead of crossing this well-trodden ground, we shall raise an issue where quiet is reigned, even among the severest informed critics who take the datahood of psychoanalysis as unproblematic. We shall show that the "data" are alloys of fact and fable that do not qualify as scientific data at all. Before taking up the absence of datahood in psychoanalysis, a few credits should be handed out.

Psychoanalysis *in psychiatry* has insisted that theses about the *mind* are important for understanding deflections of mental systems (departures from the design specifications of a theoretical ideal. See Chapter 13 on Deflections). Interest in ideas must sometimes be maintained a long time until the right reasons can be found for their acceptability. Psychoanalysis repsychologized a psychiatry that believed all mental disorders were brain diseases. But psychiatry as a profession is subject to fads. So we find psychiatry again enthusing— with better cause than in earlier years—at the hardware level, with biochemical, neurophysiologic, and genetic explanations that bypass the semantic level of representation. Psychoanalysis, however, advocates an interest in mental processes, what we call here semantic-level properties of mental systems.

Freud phrased his first model of the mind in terms of particles, motions, forces, and energies. These were physical concepts in the Helmholz tradition now considered appropriate for the hardware but not for the semantic level. Over a three year period while he was a university student, Freud took five courses (his *only* electives) in philosophy from Franz Brentano (Barclay, 1964), a philosopher famous for the thesis that mental representations were intentional, pointing to objects beyond themselves, and irreducible to the vocabulary of physics. It was Brentano who recommended Freud as the translator of the German edition of the 12th volume of John Stuart Mill's works edited by Thomas Gomperz (Merlan, 1945, 1949). Despite Freud's professed abjuration of philosophy, his transition from a particle-in-motion theory to an intentionalistic idiom was, we believe, heavily influenced by Brentano. (These historical connections deserve fuller treatment by scholars of the history of ideas.) Freud's efforts also exemplified a cherished goal of Brentano, that psychology and the philosophy of mind should become part of natural science. Freud tried to do this by appealing to clinical findings.

Freud moved from a particle-in-motion explanation to an intentional explanation in terms of internal mental representations. His second attempt at explaining the mental may not have been right, but, by current cognitive science standards, it was of the right *kind* because it was at the right level, namely, the goal-directed processing of semantically significant content. In developing a computational theory of mind, we want to understand the organization and trans- actions of algorithms at the semantic level; we leave it to others to understand the operations of electrochemical fields at the hardware/device level. From our perspective, the less an account of the former resembles an account of the latter, the better it is for higher level *psychologic* explanation.

Psychoanalysis insists on the importance of unconscious process- es, a central psychoanalytic thesis with a pre-Freud history of several centuries (Whyte, 1960). But it took a Freud to drive it home. The concept of unconscious processes has been absorbed into both folk and general psychology. The main scientific problems now concern how to characterize the specifics of unconscious, nonconscious, or transconscious processes. Though it may not be a natural carving of nature at its joints (the mind seems to be able to make it all joints), the distinction between unconscious and conscious content presents unsolved problems. These include the strategies of a mental system that purposively selects and excludes information from conscious attention and undergoes effects of this excluded unconscious activity.

> *Civilization advances by extending the number of important operations we can perform without thinking about them.*
>
> —Whitehead

Psychoanalysis also deserves credit for uncovering dead ends. This may seem a left-handed compliment to those who do not realize how much of scientific inquiry ends in the discovery of untruths and dead ends. (Hundreds of workers searched for decades for the microbes causing beriberi. There are none.) Failures provide valuable negative information. There are more ways of going wrong than right, and one has to go up an alley to find that it is blind. In our view, trying to test psychoanalytic theory with clinical findings leads to a dead end, because the "data" are not acceptable for scientific datahood. We get to that in detail in the next chapter.

As historians point out, the central ideas of psychoanalysis were discussed by 19th-century philosophers and writers interested in the mind (Ellenberger, 1970; Whyte, 1960). These efforts were considered natural philosophy *(Naturphilosophie)*, not science. For example, Carus (1789-1869), whose volumes were in Freud's library, wrote extensively about the importance of unconscious thinking, instinct, and sexual desire. Helmholz, one of Freud's idols, emphasized the role of unconscious inference. Freud tried to stake a scientific claim

for some ideas from philosophic psychology by citing clinical findings, especially success of treatment, as supporting evidence. Perhaps even believing he originated these philosophic ideas, he applied
them to conditions seen by clinical practitioners. Psychoanalysis has
faced a barrage of criticism for this move. It was revolutionary, but
was it a revolution *in science*? (Cohen, 1985). No.

> *Each sect has its truth*
> *And every truth has its sect.*

> —Chinese proverb

> *Out of all delusions we select one, one which matches us*
> *best, and we proclaim it the truth.*

> —Kazantzakis

The easiest target for criticism has been the behavior of psychoanalysts who act more as true believers than as inquirers. They have
driven legitimate science away from potentially valuable ideas by
their undisciplined methods and fictive knowledge claims. True
believers, both ideologic and theologic, champion one and only one,
sacrosanct story, protecting it against significant change and preserving the mystique. They have no disciplinary ideal, as is characteristic
of science, to modify or abandon received theories in the light of new
knowledge. Complacent ideologues and doctrinaire authorities un-
willing to take back mistakes are found in any field. Overawed by the
myth of a hero they wish to imitate (but winding up instead imitating
one another), loyal adherents find no further problems to solve
because all have been solved by the received doctrine. (For Freud as
the hero who turns out to be not so heroic, see Crews, 1986.) The
paradigm became paradogma with agreements based on ideologic
uniformity. The task for loyal adherents, then, is evangelistic: convince others of the doctrine's truth. In contrast, in authentic science
the presence of an unsolved problem implies that traditional beliefs
are in question. Obsessed with wanting to be accredited as intellectual authorities or cultural heroes, true believers present themselves
as scientists, science now being the accepted authority. Like the hero
Freud, most psychoanalysts work as lone-wolf practitioners outside
academia and the sciences. Some are convinced that in treating
patients they do science. Theirs is a Cargo Cult science, however—
they go through the apparently right motions, but the largesse never
arrives.

The most telling criticism of psychoanalysis has been that its claims
lack warranted assertibility because of the weak linkages between
theories and clinical observations, the latter being contaminated by

the influence of the psychoanalyst (Grünbaum, 1984). As we argue here, attempts at data-theory linkages are futile for a more fundamental reason: *there are no reliable data at all.* Reports of clinical findings are mixtures of facts, fabulations, and fictives so intermingled that one cannot tell where one begins and the other leaves off. These reportorial concoctions in the literature are constructed by authors in order to be acceptable to psychoanalytic audiences and journal editors. But we never know how the reports are connected to the events that actually happened in the treatment sessions, and so they fail to qualify as acceptable scientific data.

The observations of systematic inquiry (pattern-recognition judgments of expert-equivalent observers) are never completely free of inference based on background information. Observed phenomena, however theory-directed and theory-laden (but, it is to be hoped, not theory-loaded), are described in natural-kind terms that constitute an implicit classification. The terms of the description in evidential language refer to observable events that can be directly or indirectly apprehended. The description language, though theory-directed and value-laden, must be rich enough and elastic enough to allow the theory that drives it to be criticized, accommodate alternative hypotheses, be revised, and even be contradicted by corrective feedback. The descriptive terms are connected by correspondence rules to the terms of the explanatory theory. Hence, phenomena are explained *under a description.* Fields have specialized vocabularies, but within a field one must be able to distinguish descriptions of observables from descriptions of the constructs of the theory in question.

Two sources of evidence are offered for psychoanalytic theories: clinical and laboratory. The clinical evidence consists of reports by psychoanalysts working within the hermetic confines of their offices with no one looking over their shoulders to make independent checks. The reports are purportedly of observations made in the therapeutic situation—a strongly interactive, interpersonal situation far too variable and uncontrolled to qualify as a systematic setting for scientific theory-testing. A patient's productions—utterances and actions—constitute the observable events heard and seen by the lone practitioner, who then selects and records aspects of them in a mixture of natural language and a specialized vocabulary. (Tape recordings represent raw information that must first be refined by an editing process described in chapter 5. For an interesting computational model of the causal processes underlying such raw information, see Clippinger, 1977.) The observation records describe observable events in an observation language that characterizes the perceptual-judgment level, which is separable from the theoretic level. The major problem for psychoanalysis is that the records of clinical descriptions in the literature are reportorial fictives. They do not describe what actually happens in the clinical situation. Thus descriptions of the actual events are inaccessible to the public scrutiny and independent evaluation required by a science.

The crucial problem is not that patient productions are influenced by the analyst and thus contaminated, as Grünbaum has argued (1983, 1984, 1986)—charitably (or naively), assuming fidelity of Freud's case reports, which, to those in the know, are simply stories endlessly told and retold around psychoanalytic campfires—but that the authenticity of agreed-on described observations does not exist. The public observation records in the literature consist of the clinician's unconstrained idiosyncratic selections, omissions, and paraphrasings. The field offers clinicians no consensible decision rules for selecting what information to report as relevant and at what level of description to report it. Without such rules, no observational consensus can be achieved: each clinician is on his own, free to report what he likes, having no way of knowing what items to record as facts. The clinician has no way of contributing data sets to a cumulative database characteristic of a scientific field. The zero-to-low fidelity of the clinician's undisciplined observation reports is the central reason why the field is unable to make empirical progress. There has been no accumulation of new facts and no iterative cycles of feedback correction to eliminate mistakes.

We attribute this lack of empirical progress to a failure to agree (a) on ground terms and (b) on what aspects of the theory or natural-kind generalizations the observed events are instances of. Observation records in systematic inquiry consist of encoded pattern-recognition similarity judgments by competent judges. "Do you see what I see?" "Do you hear what I hear?" If the answers are yes, the judges agree; if the answers are no, something is amiss.

Observers look at a famous photograph of Einstein riding a bicycle.

1st observer: What do you see?
2nd observer: An old man on a bicycle.
1st observer: Right.
3rd observer: I see Einstein riding on a bicycle.
1st observer: Right. Isn't Einstein here an old man?
3rd observer: Yes.
4th observer: I see a famous man laughing at the absurdity of having himself photographed on a bicycle.

1st observer: But you would agree with us that it is a photograph of an old man on a bicycle?

4th observer: Yes.

Notice that the observers can resolve disagreement because the description language is rich enough to allow for contrasts as well as similarities. The observers agree on the meanings of natural-kind ground terms "old," "man," "bicycle," "Einstein," and what they similarly perceive as positive instances of these kinds. In contrast, psychoanalysts observing raw-data videotapes of clinical sessions do not agree among themselves about what is happening. In Rashomon style, each describes the events in his own way and interprets them as instances of various theoretical categories as he sees fit.

No decision rules exist for encoding what is selected as relevant from the raw information by assigning items to agreed-on natural-kind categories. Without the same manifest phenomena acquiring the same description and without agreement on the significance of patient productions describable at the observational level of immediately apprehended pattern-recognition, arguments about the adequacy of empirical support for a theory are superfluous. Without datahood, there is nothing to argue about.

Because clinical reports lack fidelity, and psychoanalysts do not agree on which observations are instances of what hypotheses, the field lacks the preliminary agreed-on data-sets essential to getting even a purely natural history phase of inquiry off the ground. The field has no principles for generating faithful observation records, and thus it cannot settle even its own disputes by appealing to comparable facts of observation. There are no data in an agreed-on observation language. Further, there are no rules that stipulate (a) what patient productions support a given hypothesis, (b) to what degree they do support the hypothesis, and (c) whether they support one hypothesis more than another. In scientific inquiry, correspondence rules, epistemic correlations, and indicator hypotheses are formulated to link observational data to explanatory theories. Explanation is relative to a data-set. But if nothing in a field qualifies for datahood to begin with, its brazen claim and refrain of being a science serves only as a self-congratulatory incantation. Psychoanalysis has no scientific credentials for its knowledge claims.

Laboratory data are a second sort of evidence for psychoanalytic theory. Here the difficulty is not that the observation reports lack fidelity, but that (a) the experimental procedures have questionable relevance to the theory and (b) the experimental results demonstrate consistency only with certain concepts and do not feed back into a modification or improvement of the theory. Erdelyi (1985), a cognitive laboratory psychologist, concludes:

> The strength of the laboratory/experimental approach, unlike the clinical, is its methodological rigor; its overriding weakness is its inability to deal with truly complex processes. Thus, none of the four critical facts in themselves are in any doubt within experimental psychology: (a) that there can be selective information rejection from awareness; (b) that aversive stimuli tend to be avoided; (c) that organisms strive to defend themselves against pain; and (d) that many psychological processes occur outside of awareness. All these facts independently are not in dispute; what is in dispute and has not been demonstrated experimentally is the conjoint fact, that is, all the component facts integrated into a higher order fact. (p. 259)

To test a theory may require as much ingenuity as to construct one. Psychoanalysis has been a permanent fad among the literati who eschew testing and who are at ease with issues requiring only words and facile argument. Like ordinary literature, psychoanalytic literature is text—no illustrations, no measurements, no tables, no graphs, no photographs, a few diagrams. But the job of science cannot be done with words and argument alone. Hands must be dirtied; one must *do* as well as *view*.

> *One must get one's hands dirty to achieve anything.*
>
> —Picasso

Given this bleak picture of a stagnating, dataless psychoanalysis, we might conclude that the field is a dead end, of no further scientific interest and deserving of oblivion. (We are not discussing psychoanalytic psychotherapy here, only the problems of psychoanalysis' claims to be a science.) Yet even its severest critics believe it is not entirely hopeless. Popper (1974) asserts that psychoanalysis "is an interesting psychological metaphysics (and no doubt there is some truth in it, as there is so often in metaphysical ideas)". He feels psychoanalytic suggestions are "psychological only." (But isn't this the kind that we want?) Bunge (1983), who considers the field a pseudoscience, says it may have one or two confirmable hypotheses in it. Grünbaum (1983) refers to "the *heuristic* value of clinical data" (without realizing there are no "clinical data") and believes that psychoanalysis provides "potential heuristic merits" (Grünbaum, 1985, p. 245), but does not venture to say what they are. In his author's response to peer commentary on his book (Grünbaum, 1984), however, Grünbaum (1986) states, "I find some empirical plausibility in the psychoanalytic theory of defense mechanisms, e.g. denial and rationalization, reaction formation, projection and identification" (p. 281). Apparently Grünbaum does not realize that it is exactly these mechanisms, specified as transformation rules, that have served as central elements in the models of computational psychology from the very start (Abelson, 1963; Colby, 1963; see Boden, 1977/1987, for a review).

> *Fundamental progress is made through the reinterpretation of basic ideas.*
>
> —Whitehead

We conclude that psychoanalysis, lacking a method for converting raw information to datal evidence, is not a science. It is a movement with a *Weltanschaung* and a *Menschanschaung* derived from the philosophy of mind. In our view, it nonetheless contains some workable (programmable) ideas that point to important aspects of human nature, particularly in the domain of extreme and enduring deflections of mental processes (see chapter 13 on Deflections). Cognitive science, computational psychology, and psychoanalysis share an interest in understanding aspects of the mind. In the pursuit phase of inquiry, in which theories are neither accepted nor rejected but explored and worked on for their possibilities, psychoanalytic ideas about mental processes should be sorted out for their initial plausibility. Winnowing the deep insights (if any) from the deep nonsense (lots), we feel most of its theoretical constructs can be jettisoned. A few can be reformulated and incorporated into a computational psychology that tries to understand human problems, including those enduring deflections, departures, dilemmas, and miseries brought on by problems in interpersonal living. By being systematically combined with ideas from other fields and becoming components of computational models with clear empirical and testable consequences, some psychoanalytic ideas may prove fruitful. A computational modeling effort must be made before one can decide. This book draws attention to and directs traffic to that effort.

Can a philosophy of mind contribute to a scientific theory of mind? Yes. (Science itself may be viewed as philosophy combined with an interventional praxis.) In contemporary cognitive science, many philosophers are doing so, for example, Dennett (1978, 1981, 1982a, 1987), Stich (1983), Brand (1984), Bechtel (1983, 1985), Fodor (1975, 1980, 1981, 1987), Haugeland (1985), Nelson (1982), Cummins (1983),

Lycan (1981, 1987), Putnam (1975), Kitcher (1985), Marras (1985), and Churchland (1984).

Inasmuch as psychoanalysts as clinicians are not scientists, what might their role be in contributing to systematic inquiry and knowledge? For thousands of years, long before there was science or scientists in the modern sense, practical men discovered and invented in agriculture, metallurgy, architecture, and navigation. Alchemists contributed valuable knowledge to chemistry, particularly when Paracelsus, in spite of his current bad press, changed their direction from seeking wealth to seeking health through the study of minerals and metals (Boorstin, 1983). Hundreds of naturalists in biology provided observational data necessary for a plausible evolutionary theory.

Psychoanalysts are practical men, artisans working to reduce mental suffering. They occupy special field-research observation posts as natural historians who can contribute descriptions of unusual patterns and their provenances necessary for a comprehensive theory of the mind and its deflections. As natural historians, psychoanalystic clinicians can observe and describe in an intentionalistic language *what is there* in the deflections and departures using intentionalistic terminology of belief, desire, expectations, feelings, and the like. The cases must be clearly described in agreed-on terms to provide iterated examples for comparison by independent others who can observe similar cases and so that similarity judgments can be quantified to see if the patterns and empirical regularities hold up. The advantage of such cases of deflections is that they are natural experiments that isolate and manipulate variables a laboratory experimenter would never think of varying, or dare to. A clinician as naturalist loses no dignity in being a field researcher charting the regularities and describing the puzzling phenomena that require better explanations than we now have. Theoretical science is not the *summum bonum* of life. There are many other activities that contribute to reliable and valuable human knowledge.

S: When Colby and I talk about psychoanalysis, we express a lot of disagreement with most psychoanalysts. (From here on, for brevity, I shall mostly say "analysts" and "analysis.") How, then, can I for over 30 years practice analysis as a therapy, use what I learn from that practice to study aspects of human behavior, and think primarily from a perspective of analytic theory? Can my enthusiasm be so mindless as to override the objections we elaborate herein? If analysis is a mess, why salvage anything; why not throw it away and get on to a more efficient, more sensible cognitive science? In this book, we express opinions about analysis that are at best mixed. But that, left as is, would not represent my experience accurately. So, to balance the scale, I want to review my positive feelings.

There are several reasons for my appreciating psychoanalysis.

1. Never before has there been such an opportunity for collecting naturalistic information on subjective experience. To reduce their unhappiness, people will talk about themselves to an analyst for hours a week, for years. They tell about their past—their myths of their past—from the beginning of memory on, and they unwittingly relive aspects of it in relation to the analyst. They reveal their secrets, past and present, they give their reasons, they invent their stories. They also tell more than they had intended and more than they know they are telling. These stories and confessions, whatever the analyst makes of them, are narrated and otherwise displayed in great detail and depth, with the feelings that accompany them marvelously complicating and enriching these presentations.

2. No field before psychoanalysis—perhaps no individual, even—has wanted to be immersed so profoundly in the study of people's subjectivity. No one before thought of doing so; no one thought it worthwhile. The ancient prescription "Know thyself" was never before applied this way. No one before, other than a few poet-dramatists, was so respectful of, even enthralled with, the most minute details of subjective life—thoughts, feelings, memories, movements, daydreams, nightdreams. There is no end to the admiration for details. No one thought that every detail counted, that every detail could have meaning, that every detail might have causes, that every detail reflected or stood for something else, that every detail was part of the natural world. And never before was such a large group of ordinary folk—we call them patients—willing to search so profoundly and persistently to find themselves.

3. No other field has tried to take every detail—any detail—and fit each to the others.

4. No other field has tried so hard to find the form, dynamics, purposes, origins, and effects of unconscious forces—both those that can, with more or less work, become conscious and those that, never conscious, can be at best only dimly made out by an observer. And no other field has had the enthusiasm, nerve, arrogance, and, at times, courage to try to systematize these unconscious aspects of subjectivity.

5. No other field saw or so appreciated the unending complexity of

the mind. And in experiencing that complexity, analysts have none-theless been drawn to find rules that ordered the dense and tangled mass of observations.

6. No other field has recognized and studied infant sexuality, the power of the drives and yearnings of infancy, the complexity and subtlety of infants' and children's minds, or the progression of childhood through observable stages of desire, conflict, and conflict resolution. No other field has appreciated and studied—again, in detail, this time by means of observational techniques that smell of science—the part infancy and childhood play in creating the struc-tures of adult identity and psychopathology.

7. No other field has tried—has respected the effort—to explore the vast territories of psychopathology: to describe them in detail; to link their origins with the forces of biology, society, the dynamics of the family from birth on, and the intrapsychic dynamics the individual creates in order to cope with these first three forces.

8. No other field has been so preoccupied with the ways and means that people falsify their integrity: the mechanisms of defense against one's inner truths (repression, disavowal, displacement, etc.), the compromise formations that let self-deception flourish.

9. No other field has so respected the power of fantasy and how it dominates mental life or insisted so unswervingly that its effects can be greatest when it is unconscious.

10. No other field has explored the intricate connections—conflicts and mediations—between biologic drives and external forces (e.g. the pressures parents apply to their children from birth on to make offspring conform) and how these struggles become internalized and fixed as permanent character structure (e.g. the voice of conscience), painful symptoms, and comfortable peculiarities of behavior.

11. No other field developed a technique, like psychoanalysis's free association and interpretation, meant to reach toward these details, conscious and unconscious.

12. No other field, except subatomic physics and perhaps astron-omy, understood that the observer shapes the field of observation and the observations themselves. And likewise for the efforts to introduce, into the techniques of observing, the study of ways to dampen the effects produced by the observer.

13. No other field adequately appreciated how the subjects (in the case of analysis, the patients) saw their relationship to the observer through the effects of their life history. No other field not only recognized the presence of these effects but saw that, in these effects, one had a firsthand experience with the patient's past (in that the patient responds to the analyst as if the latter were the major figures—

mother, father—of the past: "transference"). Therefore, no other field had the opportunity, however flawed it has been in analysts' hands, to beware taking at face value people's expressions of their subjectivity.

14. Though it is not well known outside of psychoanalysis, psychoanalysis has moved toward using a communications theory as its basic premise. Freud, late in life (1925, p. 140), without giving up some of the old vocabulary, shifted his theory of the mind from a mechanistic hydraulic model of energy (libido that invests [cathects] body parts and ideas) to an information processing theory:

> At one time I attached some importance to the view that what was used as a discharge of anxiety was the cathexis which had been drawn in the process of repression. To-day this seems to me of scarcely any interest. The reason for this is that whereas I formerly believed that anxiety invariably arose automatically by an economic process [amount of energy], my present conception of anxiety as a signal given by the ego in order to affect the pleasure-unpleasure agency does away with the necessity of considering the economic factor (p. 140).

15. Even those put off by psychoanalysis grant that it has provoked many long-lasting excitements in the world of ideas. It has not been easy to dismiss: some of those who disagree have been driven to fine work. Psychoanalysis, many grant, is certainly heuristic (see Farrell, 1981, pp. 193-194, 204-205.)

16. Freud tried to push on to a revolution in philosophy: to take the proof out of the hands of the philosopher's subjectivity and the rules of argument each school of philosophy prefers by adding careful, detailed, confirmable natural observations thereby collected beyond the observer's subjectivity. That was how philosophy became natural philosophy (our present-day word for which is "science"). To do this for the mind was Freud's daring advance. We write this book to praise the effort and mark its failure so far. (Colby spoke of this earlier with his remark that science is philosophy plus praxis.)

Whatever the failures of psychoanalysis, as practice and theory, in its efforts to be a science—and we choose to emphasize these failures herein—never before in the study of human behavior has a field been so concerned to use that essential of science, skepticism. That analysts have often not been skeptical enough is painful, confirming how even those of us forewarned have trouble escaping the baleful effects of the self-deluding mechanisms of defense described by psychoanalysts.

Farrell (1981, p. 25, and discussed at length pp. 172-173) lists attributes of analysis I admire:

1. Psychic Determinism. No item in mental life and in conduct and behaviour is 'accidental'; it is the outcome of antecedent conditions.
2. Much mental activity and behaviour is purposive or goal-directed in character.
3. Much of mental activity and behaviour, and its determinants, is unconscious in character.
4. The early experience of the individual, as a child, is very potent, and tends to be pre-potent over later experience.

In one way or another, in one place or another, with one philosopher or poet or scientist or another, one or another of the above ideas was expressed before Freud. (And it pays for analysts to recall that most of the insights we announce to our patients have already been published in the writings of philosophers, penny weighing machines, and Chinese fortune cookies.) Nonetheless, no one else pulled them together into a system—no matter how epicycled, incomplete, overgeneralized, and untestable—that tried to explain the lively, dynamic flow of human behavior. No one else tried to invent a technique to systematically collect observations on the subjectivity of an individual. No one else built into the effort to collect observations the idea that much of mental life must sometimes be approached by indirection (free association). (We only wish that Freud, in his ambition, had not hidden his debts to his intellectual forebearers—he could give credit to artists but hardly to scientists and philosophers—and, even from the grave, had not enlisted colleagues to sustain his herohood.)

Finally, we say wryly and in keeping with a basic idea in this book, no other field not a science has so wanted to be one, has so watched the behavior of the unquestioned sciences, has so struggled to make itself a science. You see Colby and me doing that now, as we predict that parts of present-day psychoanalysis can contribute to cognitive science, though what we conclude—that analysis will become something else—must displease most analysts. But if it stays where it is now, we argue, psychoanalysis cannot be a science as that word is understood in the world of science. Farrell (1981) quotes Medawar: "The opinion is gaining ground that doctrinaire psychoanalytic theory is the most stupendous intellectual confidence trick of the twentieth century: and a terminal product as well—something akin to a dinosaur or a zeppelin in the history of ideas, a vast structure of radically unsound design and with no posterity" (p. 9). We find that sentiment rather inflamed but, beneath the rhetoric, important. When we are done expressing our similar sense of psychoanalysis's weaknesses, we are left with the hope of progeny: a cognitive science one of whose ancestors was psychoanalysis. For we believe, contrary to the claim of most psychoanalysts, that the theories and findings of psychoanalysis do not constitute a science, as that word is used in most fields that psychoanalysts accept as sciences, for example, physics, chemistry, and biology. But we can see how certain psychoanalytic ideas and observations, when taken over by cognitive sciences, can become a true science of the mind. (If only analysts would realize that the question for them is not whether analysis is a science but whether — the test of any field — its statements [e.g. reports of observations] are believable.)

I shall now complain more precisely.

5

Our Science: No Reportable Data

S : Suppose I want to communicate, through written publication, something I have observed. Let it be the result of a laboratory experiment, and let the audience be professional colleagues. If the techniques in the laboratory are appropriate, familiar, and standardized, I need not even mention them beyond what would allow a colleague to imagine the setting and the procedures. With the report as a guide, he or she is free to repeat the experiment to see if my data are correct and my conclusions appropriately drawn.

Not one word of that description holds for the findings of psychoanalysis. First, the report of a psychoanalyst is hearsay, and much of the language consists of code words used to express one's identity as an analyst, one's sharing in the brotherhood, one's expertise with the rituals. Analytic reports never mention the nature of the calibrating — observing and recording — instrument: the analyst at the moment the observations were made. The reading audience agrees not to doubt that that instrument, though not described, subject to the winds of emotion, and impossible to calibrate, measures reliably.

Second, the moment of observation will never return. Neither the analyst nor his colleagues can ever, as scientists can in the laboratory (more or less, never the same in every detail), repeat the procedure.

Third, though the account comes to us from the therapist, we have no reason to believe it is more than an impression. Let us say that I take notes during the hour. What do I put down and what omit? What words do I choose, in the heat of the treatment, to describe what is happening? Would I in a different mood or state of digestion write the same notes for the same events? What goes on in me — deep tides of personality or only responses to the present — that controls my attention, my preferences for selecting what counts? How close

41

would my notes come to those the patient would write (an impossible demand on patienthood)? Suppose I do not take notes but, like Freud, write up my cases at the end of a 12-hour day—or three years later?

Now I have my notes and shall prepare a case study. What transformations shall I make in trying for coherence, style, proof of theories? What will be the relationship between what went on in the room and what goes onto the page as I write? Suppose I am an unskilled writer, not good at description? Suppose I am a skilled writer, good at description and therefore, perhaps, all too good at representing my point of view as being the truth? Suppose, as almost always happens in analytic reports, that I decide against using the language of observation, crude as it is—"the patient was sad," "the patient sighed," "the patient cried" (as if there are not innumerable forms of sadness, sighing, and crying)—and switch over to technical language—"the patient manifested a deeply regressed, prenarcissistic cathexis of the archaic selfobject," "the oral sadistic instincts displayed in the dream undoubtedly indicated that . . ."?

The report heads toward publication. Its shape is now influenced by my expectations of what editors and referees will accept. Is it part of a book written only by me; about one patient or many? Is the book put together by an editor with me just one of the contributors? If the report is submitted to a journal, which one is it and what do I know about that journal's likes and dislikes? The report is accepted for publication, and the editorial process grinds away: requests/demands for rewriting change the text. Am I famous enough to be published even if I refuse the suggestions, or must I comply?

What has become of the original moment in my office, and what reader can work backward from publication to that moment in order to detect the relationship between what is published and what happened between the patient and me?

Perhaps the reality of that moment is protected by recordings: audio or audiovisual tapes. Then, at least, the outsider knows the conversation has been preserved; despite sometimes insuperable problems of confidentiality, there is a permanent record. But it is not a record of what happened, only of what was recorded. We cannot, for instance, record thoughts or feelings. If a transcript is made, it will be at the mercy of the vagaries of recording, listening, typing, and editing. And unedited transcriptions of conversations can verge on incomprehensibility to a reader and are often unbearably dull. In the case of movies or television tapes, lights, camera placements, exposures can subtly (but nonetheless powerfully) change subliminal clues. Most painful of all, when experts look at/listen to the same recording, their interpretations of what is happening can be widely discrepant.

In brief, then, analysts' data are not dependable enough to fit the minimal standards of what the rest of the world calls science. Yet almost no one—friend or enemy—notes this lack of factualness of psychoanalytic case reports (for instance, Edelson, 1977; Grünbaum, 1984; Harrison, 1970; Holt, 1961; Joseph, 1975; Kohut, 1970; Lustman, 1963; McIntosh, 1979; Wallerstein, 1986). The discussants take that primal issue for granted and mount the attack at grander problems (e.g. Can there be a hermeneutic science? Are the hypotheses of psychoanalysis testable?).

Let me now represent that process of transforming information so that nonanalysts can have a more real experience of analytic data. There is a problem, however, in finding an example. First, nowhere in the world, allegations to the contrary, is there a published verbatim account of what a patient said, what the analyst said to the patient, what the analyst wrote in his notes during the treatment hour, what the analyst wrote later in his progress notes for the patient's file, what high-level theory statements the analyst derived from the treatment moment, and the relationship of these steps in communication to the final product, the published version of the experience ("The patient's projective identification resulted in a narcissistic cathexis of the selfobject," etc.).

Second, I cannot use an example from my work because I do not move, in writing, from the concrete to high-level theory. I can report what the patient said, what I said, what notes I took during the hour, the summary I dictated after the hour, and what I concluded therefrom. But I do not write in the psychoanalytic style and so can only simulate how that might appear, were I someone else.

Third, even if I write an accurate account of the transaction—and who but an all-knowing god could be the judge to decide what is *the* accurate account—how can the reader place that description in the context of the treatment, a relationship that may have gone on for years?

So I must invent an example. But the reader need not fear that what follows is a distortion of the way analysts write; I constructed this jargon statement from a colleague's published works. Those familiar with the analytic literature will find the following true to the form, not a parody: "In a dream were exposed the preoedipal configurations of the narcissistic rage present in the unaltered omni-science of the archaic grandiose self, which, we know, is remobilized constantly in the careful analysis of the narcissistic personality disturbances."

Now, how does the conversation go—what are the words that an analyst uses in a typical moment of analysis enroute to a summarizing conclusion like the foregoing?

The actual treatment session lasted about 50 minutes. In it were spoken several thousand words, mostly the patient's. In addition were his and my inflections and rhythms of speech; hesitations; explanations; body movements; affects clearly, dimly, subliminally, and unconsciously felt by each of us; and all the rest of the teeming mass of communications and the non-communicating noises that, along with the same movements in me, make up a moment of relatedness. Beyond that are our thoughts, conscious, preconscious, unconscious.

Let me show you a rendering from my notes, taken during a treatment hour, into the dictation that, on tape, is the record of what happened. (Even as I dictate it, my mind is full of how much has been left out and how the act of quoting conversation already modifies the material.) In the following, I use brackets for remarks added now for the reader's elucidation. Except for the report of a dream, the syntax of direct quotes has been cleaned up.

"Was I on time?" he says. He found my door open and felt it as an accusation that he was late. He talks about differences of a minute or so between his watch, the clock in my office, the clock in the outer office, other clocks in the building. I say, "What is the accusation you think I'm making?" He doesn't answer directly but instead talks of "tiny failures," such as how often he is a few minutes late here. He has two theories about today's business with time, first that the clocks and watches differ and second, that, if it means so much to him, that must be due to "resistance." He thinks now of a business deal that is starting up: he has to get three participants to join together—the board of a company, in fact one person with the power; an outside specialist to be brought in just for this job; and the group that controls the raw material. His job is to get them all to work together, but each wants one of the other two out of the deal. Why can't he be as effective as his brother, who, for all his awful mistakes in business, is getting more and more powerful assignments. He reports a dream [given here without improving the syntax and hesitations, so that the reader can get a more accurate flavor of how we talk].

PT: "Uh [pause] Uh . . . I was just . . . my brother . . . this guy at the restaurant is . . . he . . . we met there for lunch yesterday and this guy who's not the maitre d', something like that, I don't know . . . his name is . . . well, my brother always gets the best table so when I'm with him, but I got there first and this guy remembers that time . . . he's just a little Mafia bastard and just because that time. [pause] Um. Uh. [pause] Fuck him. He thinks that just because. [pause] Anyway, I ate too much. The portions were immense, and my brother said . . . besides, the food is disgusting. My father loves it. [pause] That's what my brother, he walks in 20 minutes late and still he gets the best table because. This little bastard . . . I dreamed last night . . . this is not important. I dreamed last night . . . Dr. Stoller, this is a bunch of bullshit. I dreamed last night . . . [pause] Veronica was dressed very stylishly and her hair was streaked. Naturally. She looked good. She was being nice. It was like a boutique that served martinis. And funny little hors d'oeuvres. It was her place. Then she slid down and I was fucking her. But I only had a three-quarters hardon. She withdrew. Then I saw her sitting with this guy with . . . he had long, black curly hair and I was angry because she was interested in him and not me. That's all I remember. When did you say was your vacation? [pause] Um. I. If that's the way. I was just wondering if. Well maybe. What about the dream? [pause] That last time I saw Veronica. It was two . . . three years? I was thinking about the house. I was thinking about the height of the sofa. I was thinking about the chairs that were redone. There was nothing with them. Why did I do that? I think my suit looks neat even if there's a hole in the jacket. I was going to say I'm filled with pain. Then I thought I'm thrilled to be filled with pain. To be alive. [pause] But I'm not quite where I need to be."

[I now summarize, in my words, the notes I dictate after the hour, on how the discussion proceeds.] He hates that restaurant. He hates his parents' house. His father is just a huge bull and his mother a stupid, beautiful cipher. "A representation of the heterosexual life?" "Yeah". Random talk. [Was it really random?] Then: "The beautiful men's golden hair and muscular bodies saved me from my father. Women's beauty wouldn't. Veronica. I can't imagine how women could save me." "They can't help you because you don't believe they can." "Right. And I imagine that a man could. My really being a homosexual began with the beginning of analysis, when I started cruising. . . ."

I shall not continue with the dictation of the complete treatment hour, partly because the needs for confidentiality overpower the needs of publishing this anecdote and partly because the dictation, in its original form, is probably close to incomprehensible to the reader not familiar with what has gone before in the psychoanalysis. These are data?! (The reader who doubts that my mundane report is typical should read the transcripts published by, for instance, Dahl, 1974; Knapp, 1974; and Gill and Hoffman, 1982.) The point is not that the "high-powered" interpretations and descriptions provided by colleagues are wrong. Rather, I am suggesting that my friends, too, have experiences like mine and that the high theory is not well connected to such experiences (See Peterfreund, 1983, 1986). My colleagues may very well be right in their published interpretations of their patients' minds. Our problem is that there is no way to know.

6

Our Science: Data on the Absence of Data

S : *Instruction to Reader*—This chapter is written as if its only audience were psychoanalysts, for it is based entirely on analytic writings. Nonetheless, I think the main points will be clear enough to nonanalysts, even if they miss a few poignant ironies.

Being uneducated in the other (so-called) social sciences, I have made no effort to apply to those fields what I know in detail about psychoanalysis. I suppose, however, that at the highest reaches of anthropology, sociology, political science, philosophy, and the rest (perhaps including cognitive science) are writings as spiritless, drenched in gravity, and deformed by pompous theory as any I can quote by analysts. You can decide if intimacy with analysts makes me think they have mastered this perverse style of discourse better than scholars in other disciplines and if analysts are more obsessed with being accepted as scientists than those in any other field anywhere, at any time. (In these chapters on Our-Science, I shall bear down harder than anyone has before on the failure of analysis to report data. I trust that going on at great length now will be better amortized if my complaints also afflict these other disciplines.)

INTRODUCTION

Every analyst has seen the phrase "our science" repeatedly in our literature. Most, I suspect, agree that theirs is a science, which therefore makes them scientists. There seems little left to discuss except to what part of science analysts should be assigned. I think, however, there is more; we should still be arguing. In doing so now,

I cannot speak as a philosopher of science. Though issues raised by scholars in these fields have influenced me and crop up herein, my approach is of a lower order. I shall not so much talk *about* the question of analysis as science, as is done in more rigorously thought through and philosophic papers and books, but shall present data, that is, facts. These will consist of quotations from the literature. I shall try to convince the reader by simple inundation: to give many examples, to make apparent their haphazard selection by me (i.e. I did not have to search them out), to get analysts to recall how many more they have absorbed over the years, to make manifest the kinds of rhetorical devices that substitute in these quotations for psychoanalytic data. And I shall assert that *psychoanalysis need not claim to be a science to legitimate both its process of discovery and the discoveries that resulted.*

> Our sceptic may be unwise enough . . . to maintain that, because analytic theory is unscientific on his criterion, it is not worth discussing. This step is unwise, because it presupposes that, if a study is not scientific on his criterion, it is not a rational enterprise . . . an elementary and egregious mistake. The scientific and the rational are not co-extensive. Scientific work is only *one* form that rational inquiry can take: there are many others. (Farrell, 1981, p. 46)

I offer no review of the literature, no summary of the perspectives, no technical language, no finely honed argument, no intellectual excellence, no advanced scholarship. I shall try, rather, for an assault with facts, quotations: what authors actually wrote. (No science here either. Let someone else, a scientist, count the number of times since the first analytic paper was published that analysis has been called a science and how many times evidence accompanied the appellation.) I want to undercut the reader's intellectual defenses and instead create, especially by using colleagues' words, a physical feeling like indigestion, of a bolus so large that in the future you will choke when you come on the phrase "our science." I wish I could get you to read every word of every quote herein. Slowly, no skimming, as if it were poetry, onomatopoeia; be impressionistic, for this material should be phagocytized more than contemplated. Only then will you get the full effect. Then you can laugh or cry, whatever is your style. And, on acknowledging how far we are scientifically from what analysts claim, we may move some aspects of analysis in a more scientific direction and more honestly defend the value of the nonscientific part.

In going through this process now, we must also analyze and so detoxify a part of the childhood of analysis: the identification with the

Freud who was embarrassed to be a philosopher and claimed—long after he left the laboratory—that he was still doing biology and therefore science. (The ways Freud and his intimates used for keeping us from saying analysis is not a science lead us to know it is not. In this case, a Zenlike thought: sometimes to prevent is to cause.)

Another ground rule. This chapter has a consciously constructed distortion: I present only evidence that disparages psychoanalysis as science. The evidence that analysis is a useful method of exploration (e.g., analysts have studied certain subjects as no one else has [Colby asks, What? I answer, for instance, transference and countertransference, oedipal conflict, infant psychic development, self-deception, defense mechanisms, childhood and adult erotic life], and analysts are told things told no one else) is hardly noted herein. If, in defense, a psychoanalytic colleague counters my argument by piling up statements on the value of analysis, my purpose will be defeated.

Someone writes, "It is an old foolishness to ask whether psychoanalysis is an art *or* a science" (Schwaber, 1976, p. 532). No. Another says, "I examined the perennially arising question, can psychoanalysis be a science and if so, of what kind, and found that modern philosophers of science see no real difficulty here. No methodological issues of special importance hinge on the question of where to classify it among the sciences, either" (Holt, 1981, p. 140).

These two remarks represent the position with which I disagree. Let us look in on the birth of an analyst:

> In my analysis he [Freud] one day made some interpretation, and I responded to it by an objection. He then said: "It is *un-conscious.*" I was overwhelmed then by the realisation that I knew nothing about it—I knew nothing about it. In that instant he had created in me his discovery of the powerful unconscious in our minds that we know nothing of, and that yet is impelling and directing us. I have never forgotten this reminder from him of what unconscious means. (Riviere, 1958, p. 149)

I read that and fall into a stunned silence.

Glover (1952) has already written this essay. I try again, for two reasons. First, he had little or no effect. Second, he did not collect concrete data, as I have; maybe he thought his argument was strong enough for a short paper to suffice. Will my approach work better than Glover's? Why not? Most of the points are obvious, few psychoanalysts have not thought of them themselves, and the evidence is familiar. (I pretend innocence here.) But Glover knew that 30 years ago: "I am well aware that in this brief review I have not

advanced any original arguments. Most of the views I have presented
. . . have been discussed from time to time throughout the development of psychoanalysis" (p. 409).

Probably the most complete study of these problems is
Wallerstein's (1976, 1986; Wallerstein & Sampson, 1971). His thought-
ful and scholarly work especially interests me because, over the years,
no one more than he has been aware of the issues I raise again—and
he has never doubted that psychoanalysis is a science.

I have tried something like this before, as an introduction to
Leites's (1971) devastating and yet funny demolition of the syntax of
psychoanalysis. Leites, like me, concentrated on the direct quotes
and, though it was not his intent, showed how easy it is to empty
analysis of its science. But it was no use; the book is pretty much
unseen and uncited.

WHAT IS SCIENCE?

Is it true that:

The repetition compulsion is beyond the pleasure principle?

No transmuting internalization of the idealized object had taken
place in the narcissistically invested aspects of the father imago?

The tubercle bacillus causes tuberculosis?

Souls transmigrate?

An ion has a positive or negative charge?

Mozart is greater than Beethoven?

Electricity exists?

Jung protected psychoanalysis by his support of the Nazi theory of
the Blood?

Corpses, underwear of the opposite sex, crushed feet, and dirty
sox are erotic?

War purifies the race?

Present animal forms are the product of a process of evolution?

Four houris await my ascent to Heaven?

Cathexis requires psychic energy?

Space is curved?

The positions of the heavenly bodies influence the affairs of
humans?

The sleep of the fetus is disturbed by concern over its father's introjected penis?

Freud suffered in splendid isolation?

He loves her?

She is happy?

I saw a unicorn in the forest?

Psychoanalysis is a successful treatment?

Your chronic fatigue is due to hypoglycemia?

The homosexual is unable to bind the original instinctual energies and to transform them into a potential tonic energy available for secondary process?

The nerves of God produced a spiritual voluptuousness and will soon impregnate Schreber?

Love makes the world go round?

Red is radiant energy?

What can we do and what should we do to check out these statements? (See Rubinstein, 1980, at least for the unicorn.)

The dictionary (Webster's, 1961) gives definitions and examples of "science": "possession of knowledge as distinguished from ignorance or misunderstanding;" "knowledge possessed or attained through study or practice;" "a branch or department of systematized knowledge that is or can be made a specific object of study;" "studies mainly in the works of ancient and modern philosophers;" "accumulated and accepted knowledge that has been systematized and formulated with reference to the discovery of general truths or the operation of general laws;" "comprehensive, profound, or philosophical knowledge." Some of the examples given are: "The basic tool sciences of reading, writing, and ciphering; . . . theology; . . . sport; . . . the science of evading work; . . . cards; . . . fencing; . . . boxing; . . . works; . . . formally taught; . . . at Oxford University; . . . subjects taught in one of the departments of natural science." Herein can psychoanalysis easily fit.

Any group effort to understand a subject qualifies, then, as a science. Is that acceptable? With definitions like that, why worry? Brenner (1968) says, "The subject matter of science is as broad as human experience itself" (p. 676). But are all subjects sciences? He properly says no: "It is not the subject matter, but rather one's approach to that subject matter which is distinctive and decisive" (p. 677). Or, to put it a bit differently, the way to define science is not its subject matter but what it does and how it does that.

Hard though it is to believe, in all the papers, chapters, and books I have read about this business of psychoanalysis as science, *almost no author said what he or she meant by science.* (Or by psychoanalysis, at least in a way acceptable to most colleagues; but that is another matter.) Psychoanalysts equate science with knowledge (*scire*, to know), but there must be some reason for preferring to say science: it is more laudatory. What freedom these authors granted themselves. Their argument is won before it starts. I fear that that ascription "science" is like "art," and "scientist" like "artist." The word "science," then, has no definition, no meaning. A science is nothing more than something someone claims is a science.

I think we could communicate more and propagandize less if we restricted the word science to those pursuits to which the scientific method can be applied. "Scientific method: the principles and procedures used in the systematic pursuit of intersubjectively accessible knowledge and involving as necessary conditions the recognition and formulation of a problem, the collection of data through observation and if possible experiment, the formulation of hypotheses and testing and the confirmation of the hypotheses formulated" (Webster's, 1961).

> The pattern of conduct that has developed in basic research serves to maintain what Robert Merton called the ethos of science. It involves the acceptance or rejection of reported findings of other workers on the basis of what Merton terms "preestablished impersonal criteria," and the public presentation of scientific findings (usually, and preferably, after critical review by editors and referees) so that they are available to the whole community. It also involves the social system of "organized skepticism" that subjects reported findings to constant critical review, with no assurance of finality. (Edsall, 1981, p. 11)

A problem for any discipline that has information it wants transmitted is how to get its audience to trust the information. Though there are no guarantees, scientific methods, refined over the centuries and still being refined, are the safest way to engender trust. (Note: "scientific methods," not "scientists," for a method demands argument and test well beyond what many scientists can bear. Until the altruism gene is transmitted to scientists, opposition and enemies, as much as conscience, must safeguard scientific method from scientists.)

For matters of fact, we have a hierarchy of sources of trust. Unfortunately, in most of us the capacity to trust is inversely proportionate to the trustworthiness of the source of the information; we yearn for seduction.

The source to which we most profoundly respond is Authority—scriptures, charisma, browbeating, conditioning, loveableness, brainwashing, culture.

Second, more trustworthy but less convincing is description. In the absence of displaying an actual specimen, we use photographs, other visual recordings, sound recordings, drawings, narrative.

Next is demonstration of the real thing—a single example, a sampling, or an ordered collection.

Last and least spontaneously compelling (except for those with exotic tastes) is scientific method, with its hypotheses, controls, statistical safeguards, public availability of data, retests, confirmations, postdictions, predictions, and peculiar enthusiasms.

It is not enough, if we want to trust the information of others, to accept their promise that their words are true, or their letters of reference (e.g. citations) from authorities, or their sincere desire to give trustworthy information. They may be picking our pockets if they offer as data only analogies, metaphors, anecdotes, reference to artistic compositions, paraphrases, euphemisms, and other rhetorical devices that, being hard to resist, demand trust without earning it. We psychoanalysts are hurt, bewildered, defensive, and unbelieving when our information is not trusted. Yet listen to us when we discuss—public and privately—another analyst's clinical work; how little we are convinced by each other.

DATA

Each of the excerpted phrases that follow was used by its author in referring to analytic data, but in none of these examples did the accompanying text give the data. When these quotes appear in our literature, the reader is asked to believe that the data were there and that we readers would agree that they were observations accurate enough to support—confirm—the discovery announced in the rest of the sentence and the sentences of the paragraph, paper, or book that followed.

Again, a request to the reader: read every word, even if you rebel or become bored. (Well, at least skim to sense the full measure.) Inside your irritation or wandering attention you will, on your own, discover the points I want to make in this discussion. Only when you experience your own avoidance mechanisms and irritation with me will you realize your reluctance to accept that you allow yourself to be manipulated if you accept such phrases as evidence or even promises of evidence. Reading each word, you can reexperience the marvel of humans prestidigitating. I beg you to persist. It is of no use, if you are like me, to give me a sentence or two of generalization; that kind of persuasion convinces only the convinced. But I cannot let the problem go so easily, for I feel strongly that the progress of psycho-analysis is more at risk from its deceptive language and imprecise clinical reports than from its aery theory or from our enthusiastic revealing of unsureness. (Some of the brackets in the quotes below indicate other forms such phrases took with other authors.)

The analysis revealed beyond all shadow of doubt that . . .

Recent experiences in analytic work suggest that . . .

I can only insist that psycho-analytic experience has put these matters in particular beyond the reach of doubt . . .

It seemed clear to the analyst [the author of this phrase] that. . . .

Equally inportant, the analytic work suggested that . . .

Clinical work has demonstrated indubitably that . . . [A reader might have doubts about "without doubt", but whose skepticism can withstand "indubitably"? RJS]

Psychoanalytic work with psychotic and borderline patients since Freud's time has led to the realization that . . .

Analysis of the psychodynamics reveals that . . .

X [a theory] is undeniable, since it was analytically established by Freud. . . .

Analytic reconstructions traced the origins of . . .

One might say that in a fair proportion of cases . . .

My clinical material indicated rather clearly, I thought, that. . . . He arrived at the understanding that . . .

We discovered that without question . . .

Analysis of his anal libido disclosed that . . .

Analytic investigation proved that . . .

The patient came to realize [see, understand, comprehend] that . . .

It was clear [certain, unequivocal, etc.] that . . .

We were obliged to conjecture that . . .

It now becomes clear that . . .

This was the true meaning of . . .

We have adduced analytical material in proof of all the hypotheses we put forward that . . .

We now knew [realized, found] that . . .

I was struck by the fact that . . .

We came to see that the unconscious meaning [significance, truth] for the patient was . . .

The patient's associations [material, fantasies] proved that . . .

It was easy to recognize that . . .

It was clear that the patient invariably [almost invariably] . . .

It seems quite certain that, at any rate, . . .

Of additional importance is the fact that archaic cathexes of the introjected parental imago . . .

Further explanation [to the patient, of a piece of theory RJS] showed that . . .

This established a kind of . . .

To be sure, this also indicated that . . .

There was much analytic evidence for . . .

It is true that . . .

This signifies that . . .

A probable significance—and possible importance—of this [symptom] became apparent in connection with the understanding of similar symptoms in other patients.

Note how often the authors construct their sentences so that the responsibility for a claim (e.g. the rightness of an interpretation or a theory) is shifted from themselves, in which case the reader would feel the declaration was only an opinion. "The dream," "the dream details," "the dream fragments," "the transference," "the unconscious fantasy," "the repressed material," "the finding," "the evidence," "the clinical material," "the facts," "the case," "the patient's response," "the data," "analytic reconstruction," "clinical experience," "further work"—not "I the analyst"—is the accountable agent.

Subliminal but not trivial.

Peterfreund (1986) puts it this way:

Psychoanalysts have tended to write as though the term *analysis* spoke for itself, as if the statement "analysis revealed" or "it was analyzed as" preceding a clinical assertion was sufficient to establish the validity of what was being reported. An outsider might easily get the impression from reading the psychoanalytic literature that some standardized, generally accepted procedure existed for both inference and evidence. Instead, exactly the opposite has been true. Clinical material in the hands of one analyst can lead to totally different "findings" in the hands of another. . . . (p. 128)

The analytic process—the means by which we arrive at psychoanalytic understanding—has been largely neglected and is poorly understood, and there has been comparatively little interest in the issues of inference and evidence. Indeed, psychoanalysts as a group have not recognized the importance of being bound by scientific constraints. They do not seem to understand that a possibility is only that—a possibility—and that innumerable ways may exist to explain the same data. Psychoanalysts all too often do not seem to distinguish hypotheses from facts, nor do they seem to understand that hypotheses must be tested in some way, that criteria for evidence must exist, and that any given test for any hypothesis must allow for the full range of substantiation/refutation (p. 129).

Here is a shower of vagueness out of which our-science is constructed:

This situation *may* lead to various autoerotic habits which are intensified in the anal-phallic period. This *may* begin early—towards the end of the first year or the beginning of the second. They *seem possibly* to blend with or displace the purer form of the transitional object according to the degree of infantile anger which has resulted from interferences with the expansiveness of growth. Even under favourable conditions, however, *some degree of* frustration is inevitable in the process of separation from the mother. Such auto-erotic activities as *may* develop in situations of severe deprivation and frustration are more constricted and less plastic in form than is true in the case of the uncomplicated transitional object. They betray their more focal defensive function in expressing tension and assume *more or less* automatized patterns. Even when an object outside the body has been selected its form and use are more concretized, and *may* take on the character of an *infantile fetish* [author's italics this last only]. Mild frustration, of course, *may* aid rather than interfere with the process of individuation, and promote autonomous functioning. (Italics added to emphasize uncertainty, lack of data.)

Those who argue that this is not typical of psychoanalytic writing are wrong. Those who say that it is in the nature of the work that we must show uncertainty or we would be falsifying our experience are right; the honest analyst can do nothing else. Rhetorical question: what does that imply and predict?

Harty (1986) demonstrates how uncommunicating is a report given in psychoanalytic jargon:

Imagine yourself for a moment as a therapist who has referred a patient for psychological testing in the hope of getting some information that will help you plan and conduct the treatment. Your patient is a 30-year-old man who complains of severe anxiety attacks, yet his behavior during the initial interview is guarded, stiff, and unrevealing, leaving you puzzled about the nature of his concerns and what the anxiety may mean. The psychological test report reads:

The patient's obsessive-compulsive facade is crumbling under the impact of intense oral-aggressive impulses. His preferred defenses of intellectualization, reaction formation, and isolation of affect are badly strained, and more primitive projective mechanisms are now visible, especially under conditions of reduced external structure. There is an occasional intrusion of primary process material into his conscious thinking, and it is likely that occasional outbursts of poorly modulated affect may occur. Although probably a man whose relationships have always been distant, he now shows increasing signs of withdrawal and weakened cathexis of reality. His failing ego functions leave him increasingly vulnerable to sadistic fantasies and panic attacks that may result in impulsive action. (p. 456-457; see also Peterfreund, 1986, p. 128)

Who doubts that the following report—a complete presentation; no more than this is told—is acceptable analytic data:

A thirty-two-year-old man has been a compulsive voyeur during his high school and college years. His central screen memory was that for many years from age three he would sneak to his older sister's bedroom door, peep through the keyhole, and watch her undress. He was convinced that his sister, as well as his parents, whose bedroom opened from the passage leading to his sister's room and whose door was always open, were aware of his activities and condoned the behavior because they "loved me." [All right so far; a clinical sketch. But watch how, next, in explaining, the author shifts to the our-science technology.]

Transference material gradually indicated that he was desperately trying to establish that his sister had a penis. Severe anxieties that developed in the transference pointed in the direction of the fantasy of the phallic woman as the source of his perversion. However, further work in analysis revealed regressions and states of confusion derived from earlier traumatic experiences of observing parental intercourse. These experiences provoked in him fusions and bisexual identifications with the mating parents.

As Colby says, psychoanalytic rhetoric is for communion, not communication.

PUFFERY

As part of the scientific aesthetic—that is, the author's effort to transfer to the reader the feeling that the writing is firm, controlled, objective, a reflection of the underlying science—personal pronouns are avoided; the passive tense is used (as in this sentence); words with several syllables are preferred to their shorter synonyms; pseudoquantitative modifiers like "very" and "some" are used, not for literary effect, but to give the illusion that measured quantities are in hand; nontechnical words are given new meanings (such as "libido," "narcissism"); and neologisms (such as "cathexis") invented to fill gaps in knowledge with scientific scraps that give us a "false legitimacy" (Breger, 1981.)

> The creation of libidinal pleasure through excitement and discharge associated with age-appropriate stimulating activities for the purpose of relieving narcissistic tensions is, of course, a well-known ubiquitous phenomenon. Sometimes, when a mother is unable or unwilling to soothe her infant's disturbed narcissistic equilibrium by an intimate response that might restore the narcissistic harmony, she may choose to substitute oral libidinal pleasure by popping a pacifier, well named, into his mouth. Adults follow a similar psychological path when they attempt to calm their sleep-preventing restlessness before going to bed by orally ingesting [the unwashed used to say "drink"] a glass of milk or a more potent nightcap or even a barbiturate.

Whenever you think, believe, imagine, fancy, have a hunch, or guess, increase your persuasive power by introducing your opinion with "I submit that. . . ."

Popper (1971) quotes Ramsey: "The chief danger to our philosophy, apart from laziness and woolliness, is scholasticism, . . . which is treating what is vague as if it were precise" (p. 9). Within the space of a single paper on sublimation appear the following terms and phrases, each of which has its own meaning or nuance distinct from, though related to, all the others. While you read this list, try to suggest tests that can be applied so that one can distinguish these different conditions and processes. (Are these next phrases just metaphor or an effort to be scientific by leaning concretely on physics?): "Desinstinctualization of libido"; "neutralization of libido"; "desexualization of libido"; "desexualized energy"; "sublimated energy"; "neutral energy"; "neutralized energy"; "primary ego energy"; "secondary autonomy"; "libidinal decathexis"; "desinstinctualization of drive energy"; "displacement"; "identification"; "reaction formation"; "the principle of change of function"; "sublimation *in statu nascendi*"; "concrete sublimatory achievement"; "noninstinctual mode of energy"; "sublimated energy"; "aim-deflected strivings"; "change in the mode of cathexis" [mode of cathexis?!]; "energy transformation"; "desaggressivized energy"; "instinct fusion"; "capacity to neutralize aggression"; "desinstinctualization of both aggression and libido"; "desinstinctualized character of the mode of energy used by the ego"; "a continuum of gradations of energy, from the fully instinctual to the fully neutralized mode"; "countercathexis"; "neutralized libidinal and aggressive cathexes"; "resistivity to regression and instinctualization"; "a reservoir of neutralized energy"; "*ad hoc* neutralization"; "'energy flux' defined as 'the transitory changes in energy distribution and redistribution such as the temporary and shifting reinforcement, of sexual, aggressive or neutral energy as it may occur in the course of any type of activity'" [remember: what you will be observing, as you attempt to test and define, is a live person with whom you are intimately communicating]; "whether, generally, in neutralization object libido must first be transformed into narcissistic libido"; "reaction formations . . . (and for that matter, all countercathexes) work not with instinctual but with some shade of neutralized energy"; "it is not unlikely . . . that the nondefensive ego activities have a higher discharge value than the countercathexes"; "reserves of neutralized energy that can be shifted [by whom? by what? who is the master of all these energies?] to where it is needed"; "the discharge aspect of neutralization"; "noninstinctual sources of neutralized energy"; "the neutralized cathexis of aims of the ego".

We do not know and cannot define, by using the findings of physics, chemistry, or biology, "psychic energy", "cathexes", "instincts/drives", "discharge", or any of the rest of these physicalist terms. Analysts do not agree on the definitions even when a physics vocabulary is not used. Some authorities do not even believe (except for drives), that these "things" exist. Just what, then, did that exercise on sublimation, from which I quoted, accomplish?

An author manages to get the following into three paragraphs of text: "archaic objects cathected with narcissistic libido", "the archaic self", "archaic grandiose self configurations", "archaic, overestimated, narcissistically cathected objects"; "these archaic configurations"; "the archaic structures", "their archaic claims", "these archaic configurations" [again]; "cohesive idealized archaic objects", "irreversible disintegration of the archaic self", "narcissistically cathected archaic objects", "reactivation of the archaic structures." Plus one "ancient structures."

You may feel he surpasses that when in one paragraph he tells of "narcissistic personality disorders", "less stable narcissistic configurations which belong to the *stage of narcissism*", "narcissistic personality disorders" [again], "cohesive narcissistic configurations", "the narcissistic 'object' "; "the narcissistic 'subject' "; "narcissistic libido", "(narcissistically perceived) psychic representation"; "narcissistically cathected", "narcissistic transference amalgamation", "pathogenic narcissistic areas of the personality". (Nowhere in psychoanalysis is there agreement among experts, from Freud on, about what narcissism is.)

In metapsychology one talks of the dynamic viewpoint and the economic (quantitative, as in the amount of "force" in a drive). It sounds so scientific. But dynamics are motives that people experience as scripts—performed, spoken, dreamed, felt. We experience dynamics in no other form. To talk of psychic energy, cathexis, discharge, libido, neutralization, is to pretend to have already discovered the physical forces and laws that underly our observations (i.e. the scripts). So to write "cathexis" is to make the reader accept our rumination as if it were a (testable) hypothesis. That, for me, is hubris, the sin of metapsychology. (For analytic colleagues: I do not use "metapsychology" as synonymous with "theory" but only the psychoanalytic theory-making that depends on a belief in the reality of psychic energy. We cannot do without theory.)

An author writes of "tender object cathexis". Why does he choose that phrase rather than "tenderness"? How does "cathectic constancy" differ from "constancy"? I feel manipulated when "castration anxiety" becomes a synonym for "fear". Think on the following epigrams (Zukav, 1980):

> Most of the fundamental ideas of science are essentially simple, and may, as a rule, be expressed in a language comprehensible to everyone. (Einstein and Infeld, 1938, p. 27)

> Even for the physicist the description in plain language will be a criterion of the degree of understanding that has been reached. (Heisenberg, 1958, p. 168)

> If you cannot—in the long run—tell everyone what you have been doing, your doing has been worthless. (Schrodinger, 1951, pp. 7-8)

If we did not believe in identification, role models, or rationalization, we might say that this almost universal idiosyncrasy of analytic communication is just a habit. A person trained to look for defensive postures, however, might suspect that an unpleasant insight is being denied. "The patient masturbated in childhood, for which he was scolded by the mother." *The* mother! Not "his mother." Analysts are so debilitated by chronic exposure to this leaden style that in relief and gratitude we think writing is good when it is nothing more than clear.

But what is the difference, as long as the data and ideas are valuable? (A newly discovered moon of Saturn is unchanged no matter how tasty the report of it.) There are two reasons. First, most people, including analysts, read less of the analytic literature than they would if it were written more simply. Second, the reader may suspect that the murky writing hides murky thinking, with the nasty possibility that the writer knows he is covering up his murky mind.

A few examples serve as reminders. An analyst may recognize in these following Valsalva maneuvers the same efforts found on most pages of published psychoanalysis for decades past. (When I am about to write in this manner, I now realize, I start puffing up inside like a blowfish.) Should you deny my irritation, please do not allege that the following lard is exceptional or that I had to search for examples. Rather, they surfaced while I, working on another matter, was reading a colleague who has taught us more than almost anyone else in the last generation. (My problem is not with the ideas but the our-science style). The quotes are all from that paper.

". . . more than ordinarily under the influence of aggressive drives." How much would "ordinarily" be? What precisely—what observations, undescribed—underlie "under the influence of"? What are "aggressive drives"—everyone seems to know but I—and what were their particular manifestations in this case? What amounts and kinds are being referred to in the "more" of the phrase "more than ordinarily"? In these words, then, is a mass of imponderables so great that only a believer can read it comfortably.

". . . a rather inadequate resolution of the oedipus complex." How much is "a rather inadequate" resolution? How does "a rather inadequate" amount differ from "an inadequate amount? What were the actual occurrences and observations thereof summarized so dimly in the word "resolution"? Remember: on the answers to such questions hang decisions about diagnoses; dynamics; etiology; treatment; recommendations for social engineering; laws of physics, biology, and psychology; and proclamations about our science.

". . . a fairly normal out-cropping of fetishism." Again, the question of quantity. How much was "a fairly normal" amount as compared to "a normal" amount? Is it about the same with fetishism as with apples, shale, horses, pigeons, or ears? What is an "out-cropping"? To what living experience the observer had in the office does that term refer? What are the criteria for "normal"? And if I cannot know to what the author is referring, then what am I to do with the rest of the paragraph in which that phrase is embedded?

". . . some tendency to abortive forms of transvestism." How much is "some"? "Tendency" already has an unmeasurable quality to it, and so what am I to make of the increasing uncertainty when "tendency" is further diffused by "some"? Does our colleague say more by adding "some"? What is "an abortive form" of anything, not to say transvestism? "Abortive" can serve the same intellectually (as well as diagnostically, philosophically, and morally) weasely purposes that got us into decades of trouble from the word "latent", as in "latent psychosis."

". . . to some extent." How much? Even if you give me the measurements of a certified, USDA "extent," I shall be lost when you tell me this is not a standard "extent" but rather a "some extent."

". . . a varying degree of development."

"This may be somewhat similar to the way. . . ."

Can you see how verbiage is used to make us (and the author) believe that precise enough measurements are in hand to support convincing generalizations on an aspect of human behavior? Since this style is the ordinary manner of communication among analysts, we really should be more diffident in accusing nonanalysts of unjustly accusing us of being unscientific.

"I would have only two relatively slight modifications of this statement. . . ." And so on.

Let us not bedevil that paper further, especially when the author is trying harder than most to be honest about the uncertainty inherent in the observations that underlie psychoanalytic concepts and issues. (We of course need words like "further", "especially", "harder", "most", "uncertainty", "inherent", and "of course" in order to express our opinions. Just don't include them in our-science.) Let us instead sadly remember how these typical phrases have been used to create, across thousands of pages and almost a century of years, the trust and conviction that our-science exists.

How weak must the ego be before we can talk of ego weakness? Set up a way to do the measuring. (By the way, what is the ego? If it cannot be defined by nonmetaphoric, observable attributes, how can its strength or weakness be assessed?) How narcissistic must we be before we are narcissistic? Or borderline? Lacking in self-esteem? With shallow values? With low self-awareness? With inadequate motivation? Imagine, then, the subliminal impression such writing gives and the sumliminal manipulation of one's own intellect required not to hear what is being said. "Heightened significance"/"significance"; "considerable overstimulation"/"overstimulation"; "fully sufficient"/"sufficient"/"enough"; "more irresistible/"irresistible"; "all too familiar"/"familiar"; "very strong fixation"/"strong fixation"/"fixation".

When an analyst, in a clinical description that is to confirm a theory, uses words such as the following, do we know what is meant? Are we not expected to believe they strengthen the argument, add weight to the evidence, make the premise scientific? *When no data are given*—no numbers, no measurements on any scale—what do these otherwise useful words mean: more, less, many, some, most, immense, significant, highly significant, very, few, discernible, considerable, numerous, inordinate, persistent, recurring, almost, rare, rather rare, by no means rare, not infrequently rare, it is more than likely that, severe, intense, extraordinary, truly extraordinary, and so on. (Let me briefly undertake to essay a try at attempting, in a rather small yet not totally insignificant way, a perhaps not completely exaggerated example: ". . . not at all infrequently rare, in fact, perhaps, often possibly not at all infrequently rare, even bordering on common.") In this way, supposedly, the demand to honor the economic viewpoint in metapsychology is met.

On and on. And never the data that could let the audience also judge whether an occurrence is, as the author says, massive, extraordinary, usual, normal, influential, mitigating, contributory, or significant. Arguments are won by means of sentence structure.

This quantifying language is perfectly fine (there: "perfectly fine") if used for style, for impressions, for impressing, with the understanding among the parties that the purpose of the communication is not exactness but rhetoric, style. There are more ways to convince— even to tell the truth—than with mathematical precision. One hundred million weighty words do not fill an ounce. But.

To qualify as work that can be called "science," need there be a quantifiable element? If so, need there be a vocabulary to communicate from observer to audience the precise amounts of the quantities? Is it still science if the element to be quantified and the measurement technique be forever secret? Must the elements to be measured be capable of measurement (e.g., weight versus fear, temperature versus psychic energy, length versus cathexis)? In naturalistic observation (a necessary precursor for much of the activity of the sciences) can we take the explorer's word—description—for what he observed? Should not a few other parties take a look also?

What does this mean: "There was excess anxiety in the ego"? Or this (same author): "The fact that too much masochistic cathexis of this position led to terror of being penetrated was very obvious in her dreams." Is it a fact? How much is too much masochistic cathexis?

What is cathexis and with what instrument in the treatment situation
was it measured? Is a position an attitude, a perspective, a complex?
If so, it is not an it but an intricate meshing of fantasies and therefore
unquantifiable. Would another observer see terror or something less,
such as anxiety? Who is the rightful judge of the clinical disagreement? How much more obvious is "very obvious" than "obvious"?
Dreams are strange communications; whose interpretation is right?
(By the way, how does masochistic cathexis differ from masochism
[whatever *that* is]?)

My complaint, I repeat, is not with the syntax of uncertainty;
another style might be dishonest. What pains me is how rarely we
express the full measure of our unsureness, how gracelessly the
unsureness appears, and how it can repeat and repeat and repeat, in
sentence after sentence and paragraph after paragraph, and yet allow
for a switchover into the most positive, declarative statements. I think
we use oracular thundering to drown out the soft sounds of uncertainty that show us and our audiences how little we know. What is
the function of this junk language if not to make an unsupported
claim for knowledge, truth, accuracy, reality? That really is a shame,
for it puts in doubt what we do know and makes it seem to everyone
but us that we yell "science" to dismiss our own doubts of the value
of what we do. We bewitch ourselves.

Over and over, and over and over appear words like "our science"
in the papers and books of analysts. I have not counted how often,
but the phrase occurs over and over. As Silverman and Wolitzky
(1981, pp. 321-322) note, does any other profession or intellectual
discipline say "science" so much? Here are building-blocks, from the
writings of psychoanalysts, for "the edifice of science". In a six
months' period, using only the four psychoanalytic journals to which
I subscribe, association newsletters, and a dozen or so books, I found
hundreds of examples. (In many of the sentences, if "science",
"scientific", and "scientifically" is removed, the meaning of the
sentence is the same):

the science of analysis, scientific laws, scientific method, scientific
activity, scientific accuracy, this new and unique science, human
science, the science of Man, the Science of man, the scientific
awakening, investigative science, realm of science, scientific paper,
the usual scientific paper, scientific presentation, valuable scientific
contribution, our scientific ranks, an explanatory science [as opposed
to non-explanatory sciences?], an explanatory science which could
prove things, the philosophy of the science of psychoanalysis, for
scientific use/usage, natural scientific psychology, scientific tradition,

scientific discourse, scientific needs of our field, scientific knowledge in our field, scientific publication, scientific enterprise, scientifically conscientious, experimental science, scientific research, valid scientific research in psychoanalysis, scientific problems, acceptable scientific framework, scientific theory, scientific explanation, scientific understanding, scientific sophistication, high-level scientific abstractions, scientific discovery, scientificity, scientific undertaking, scientific opinion, scientific attitude, scientific exchange, scientific loci, scientifically warranted, scientific justification, scientific outlook, creative science, scientific life, scientific doctrine, scientific correlation, scientific endeavors, scientific work, scientific progress, scientific verification, scientific argument [process of logic], a scientific study of the case, quite scientific, very scientific, scientific program [three usages: meeting, overall research plan, political activity], an interpretive and an objective scientific discipline, psychoanalysis as a scientific discipline, a scientific type of theory, scientific congress, scientific standards, scientific values, scientific conceptual framework, the usual [?] scientific framework, within the framework of what is currently known scientifically, scientific psychoanalytic contributions, a contribution to the science of psychoanalysis, scientific foundations, scientific manner, scientific ethos, scientific ethical standards, scientific status, substantiated (and agreed upon) scientific status, scientific metapsychology, scientific argument, scientific truths, scientific approach, scientific ideology, scientific scrutiny, scientific study, scientific stand [position], scientific means [nonfinancial resources], scientific liabilities, scientific objectivity, scientific paradigm, scientific field, this field of science, our field of scientific work, scientific utility, scientific commitment, scientific form, scientific symbolization, scientific terms, scientific purposes, scientific responsibility, a scientific psychoanalysis, the heart of science, the mold of science, hermeneutics, the art or science of interpretation, a science of meanings, cultural sciences, scientific clarity, scientific background, scientific grounding, modern scientific basis, scientific spirit, scientific spirit of inquiry, scientific thinking, scientific thought, meaningful scientific research, scientific gains, simultaneously clinically and scientifically relevant, natural scientific psychology, scientific view of the world, the science of the mind, scientific edifice, scientific debate, scientific career, scientific task, applied science, scientific conclusions, scientific conceptualizations, scientific character [i.e., quality], our traditional science and road to science as bequeathed to us by Freud, the study and advancement of psychoanalytic science as founded and developed by Sigmund Freud, our current and ongoing scientific march, the scientific use of the 'peculiar', our science *qua* science, respectable and appropriate science, a descriptive science, in a state of 'normal science' (Kuhn), scientific world-view carried on by a scientific community, our ordained future course as a science, our crucial scientific tasks ahead, our domain as science, the serious stamp of science, that stamp of science, the science of the inner world, a structural science, a comprehensive scientific theory of the mind, an evolved, explicit scientific theory, our psychoanalytic scientific task, the kind of science that the psychoanalytic endeavor creates for us, our peculiar science, an objective and scientific attitude, scientific predilections, scientific rigor, scientific purview and prestige, scientific validation, metapsychology may be a branch of natural science, a branch of science, the new science, our new science, further scientific advance, further development of the science, a specialist science, a clinical science, one unified science, a developing science, poetic science, a sound scientific basis, systematic scientific scrutiny, sound and scientific clinical theory, a unified science of human behavior, scientific journals, scientific content of journals, the scientificity of psychoanalysis, scientific forums, scientific media, scientific nature, the scientific function of Freud's hypotheses, vigorous scientific thinking, scientific methods of thinking, psychoanalysis as the science of man, this process of scientific assessment, scientific aims, scientific system, scientific potential, scientific growth, scientific insight, scientific findings, scientific complexity, scientific simplicity, scientific inference, scientific difficulties, scientific comprehensiveness, scientific work in analysis, a firmer scientific footing, interpretation as a valid scientific procedure, scientific value of an interpretation, scientific reconstructions, scientific productivity, scientific production [two usages: a product such as a paper; a process or capacity that massively bears fruit], scientific implications, implications for science, scientifically serviceable, scientifically fertile, scientifically validated, scientifically speaking, scientific objectivication, scientific discipline [two usages: field, rigor], scientific labour, scientific controls [as in isolating factors for an experiment] psychoanalytic scientific activities, scientific observations, adequate scientific observation, scientific empathy, the science of introspection, depth psychology and the other sciences, the science of the study of metapsychology, psychological (psychoanalytic) science, psychological science (in its own right) and in its place among the array of sciences, psychoanalytic scientific research.

Who would deny that the analytic literature is full of that vocabulary? In the space of an 11-page paper (on empathy, not on analysis as science), Kohut (1983) gives us the following, all in reference to analysis: "The essential simple and clear scientific message", "scientific pursuits", scientific sobriety", "scientific rigour", "scientific hypothesis", "the scientific 'high road' ", "decisive scientific action", "substantial intrinsically scientific grounds", "less of a science and more of a moral system", "less of a scientific procedure . . . and more an educational procedure", "the depth-psychological scientist's perception", "all my scientific colleagues", "a phase of scientific working through", "the scientific road I have been following", "spurred me toward scientific action", "falling within the domain of the natural sciences", "his scientific system", "its scientific results", "nonscientific, perhaps", "the two universes accessible to science . . . the sciences which explore the fields that are accessible via extrospection: the physical and biological sciences. And the sciences which explore the fields that are accessible via introspection: psychoanalysis *par excellence*." He uses "science" and "scientific" nine more times.

Is there any other subject, discipline, practice, or art that keeps nattering on about being a science? [C: Yes. Parapsychology.] Certainly none of the fields the rest of the world considers sciences. I hardly ever see "science" in the scientific reports of the journal *Science*, even though it is published by an association that wants to advance science.

Do we want to sound like this?

From a Declaration by Pavel Filanov, 1923: "I completely reject as unscientific all dogmas in painting from the extreme rightists to the Suprematists and Constructionists together with all their ideologies. Not one of their leaders can paint, draw, or understand in analytical terms what, how, and why he paints" (Barron & Tuchman, 1980).

We talk of *the* unconscious rather than using "unconscious" as an adjective (e.g. "unconscious thoughts", "unconscious motives"); *the* ego rather than "ego functions". We initiate and commence, seldom start; reiterate but seldom repeat; enumerate, not list; demonstrate and give evidence rather than show; terminate and conclude rather than end; decathect but not disconnect. A piece of work is efficacious, not just effective; what a peasant says he can use, an analyst finds to have utility or be utilizable. Arguments increase their potency by acquiring thrust. "He had some suspicions" is better science than "He suspected" or "He thought" or "He guessed"? Who would trade "We find it is permissible to hypothesize that . . ." for "perhaps"? "I took cognizance of the fact" beats "I was aware." "It is incumbent upon us," not "We ought." Many words are better than less; more syllables are better than fewer; neologisms are better than common words.

Words drawn from the natural sciences are the best; though they start humbly as metaphors, they soon transmute our ideas into true science. We use odd locutions, such as "It came to be understood," so that we do not have to make clear in our report that *we* made the interpretation to the patient, who never really understood it but just acquiesced and in that way made us almost aware we did not really understand either. To admit that the proofs of our treasured theories are so precarious would ruin the our-science we have built in us.

Fustian; bombast (perhaps even fustianistically bombastical, if not vice versa); orotundity, platitudinous ponderosity, polysyllabic profundity, pompous prolixity, rodomontade.

Certainly, this may be possible. It is of no small significance, after all, that there may arise the possibility that . . .

Does anyone consciously record these devices? We absorb them "unthinkingly" as we read, and so did the referees for the journals and books that accepted these writings. This gabbling is our model, our disguise, an illness. I am so used to it that I have to throw a switch in my head ("hypercathexis") in order to notice. Analysts are so forgiving (of ourselves, at any rate). Surely, you say, these rhetorical devices are only stylistic or metaphoric. Surely they are, not to say, in addition: without doubt, indeed, of course, unquestionably, positively, absolutely. And also obviously, assuredly, definitely, decidedly, clearly, unequivocally, unmistakably, undoubtedly (if not indubitably) undeniably, indisputably, incontestably, incontrovertibly, irrefutably, doubtlessly, by all means (perhaps even by all manner of means), in all events, make no mistake about it, and beyond the shadow of a doubt. For, when all is said and done, it goes without saying.

Freud, by his example, gives those who follow, permission to rattle like that. Freud (1905/1953): "No doubt it is conceivable that there may also be . . ." (p. 236).

If psychoanalysis is a science, how shall one deal with these next statements to check their correctness? (The issue now is not whether an idea is true, but how, in the form it is stated, it can be tested.)

> The phantasy attacks [by the infant of a few months of age] on the mother follow two main lines: one is the predominantly oral impulse to suck dry, bite up, spit out and rob the mother's body of its good contents . . . the other line of attack derives from the anal and urethral impulses and implies expelling dangerous substances (excrements) out of the self and into the mother.

Or:

The pleasure principle seems actually to serve death instincts.

Or:

If . . . the mother's responses are grossly unempathic and unreliable, then the gradual withdrawal of cathexis from the imago of the archaic unconditional perfection is disturbed; no transmuting internalization can take place; and the psyche continues to cling to a vaguely delimited imago of absolute perfection, does not develop the various internal functions which secondarily re-establish the narcissistic equilibrium— either (a) directly, through self-soothing, i.e., through the deployment of available narcissistic cathexes; or (b) indirectly, via an appropriate appeal to the idealized parent—and remains less relatively defensive vis-à-vis the affects of narcissistic injuries.

Or:

The plasmic orgone energy functions in the living organism as specific biological energy. As such, it governs the total organism and expresses itself in the emotions as well as the purely biophysical organ movements. Thus psychiatry, for the first time and with its own means, had found roots in objective natural-scientific processes.

Or:

After a thorough examination of the Unconscious, its psychical content and complicated mechanism of conversion into the conscious, by the analysis both of abnormal and of normal people, we have come up against the final origin of the psychical unconscious in the psycho-physical, which we can now make biologically comprehensible as well. In attempting to reconstruct for the first time from analytic experiences the to all appearances purely physical birth trauma with its prodigious psychical consequences for the whole development of mankind, we are led to recognize in the birth trauma the ultimate biological basis of the psychical. In this way we gain a fundamental insight into the nucleus of the Unconscious on which Freud has constructed which may claim to be comprehensive and scientific.

Should you think these phrases are unfairly excerpted, here is a series at full sentence length (not the scraps quoted earlier), all from one paper. We are to trust these declarations, for no data are given. (How could they be?)

It was clear that he invariably employed the same method of ego defense in a situation in which he was in danger of losing a good object, and that was to internalize the experience which stimulated the anxiety and introject the lost object. . . . *It was possible in this patient's case to recognize* different forms which the necessity to incorporate and have control over the parents could take, *and to show how* the infantile sadism was bound up with the necessity to have control over the parents and their imagos, and in this way to take part in their sexual relationship. . . . *The analysis showed that* the sexual wishes were not separate from the fulfillment of death wishes, and while *it was clear that* there was a strong libidinal attachment to the parents, *it was equally clear that* the aggressive component had come to dominate the unconscious situation, *and that* the inhibitions and restrictions of the ego were bound up with the persistence of an unconscious sadistic game which involved the destruction of the love objects or his own castration. . . . (italics added)

My complaints here may be obvious; that quote is forty years old. Where, then, is the literature by analysts (so many of whom freely concede they are scientists) that complains of this kind of writing? I can think offhand only of Leites (1971) and a paper by Slap and Levine (1978).

Is this a metaphor or a belief in a true energy?

The spreading of cathexis on objects, functions, and aims somehow or other related to the original ones is in fact part of the primary process. Thus the ego, and already the precursors of the fully developed ego, becomes invested with drive energy.

Because of the *active persistence of primary identification* to an *unusual degree,* the fetishist feels castrated when he is directly confronted with the female genital area. (italics added)

What does "active" mean? What would be inactive persistence? What is the actual form of the behavior—the psychologic experience—that is judged as possessing persistence? What is identification and what are the observations that make one differentiate primary identification from other forms? What is an unusual degree as different from a usual degree of persistence?

"There generally seems to be a definite disturbance," writes the same author. What range of quantity does "generally" encompass, especially when it is a measurement described by "seems" rather than "is"? What instructions should we follow to distinguish "a definite disturbance" from one that is only "a disturbance"?

It has seemed to me that this is the *nucleus* of the *most severe* criminal perversions expressed in violence: that *true and full* genital pleasure rarely develops. Genitality *may be* abandoned altogether in favor of narcissistically driven aggressive orgies. [I'd hate to join a non-narcissistically driven, nonaggressive orgy.] Or it *may* continue a wavering and uncertain course with homosexual and other perverse patchwork to sustain its *phantom* quality, which *may* also be expressed in a *symbolic,* displaced, *inverted way* through the use of weapons for violence. *Strong oral drives may be seen* directly or in disguised forms in the *devouring quality* of the *general aggression.* The grandiose "love" is the love of conquest, with a vision of world-wide notoriety or world-wide domination, a desire that *to some extent* is *further determined* by the *contribution* of the preadolescent years. (italics added)

By now the point is obvious. But not stunningly obvious. More quotations are needed for stunning the reader—into acute decathexis, archaic narcissistic reactivated secondary vicissitude, or a tormented admission that these samples typify the cream of analytic writing.

The assumption that this universal primal fantasy is reinvested at puberty is made *very plausible* by the *frequency* of such early adolescent practices as hiding the penis between the thighs and the attempts at autofellatio. Moreover, *there are cases* in which a perversion, such as transvestism, or the choice of transvestite sexual objects, becomes overt in middle age; *such cases again confirm* that the fantasy had lain dormant in the id and became reinvested under the impact of fresh traumata, which invariably constituted a severe castration. (italics added)

No evidence given. What are the dimensions of the id (which Freud described as dimensionless) that a fantasy (an ego product) can lie inside it?

Sometimes in cases of impotence we hear this fantasy expressed: "If the woman's body were transparent so I could convince myself with my eyes that my penis is still there, I would be potent!"

I would certainly like to know how many times those "sometimes" occurred. (Can you tell, from that quoted sentence, if the fantasy is expressed by the patient or the analyst quoting what he said to the patient?)

The part of me that is trained analyst reads dozens of analytic papers and books each year and, in searching for information, absorbs these sentences. I subliminally translate the words into my own experience, direct with patients and indirect from years of reading. But when I use a different head, when I am not just an interested reader but a nag who wants exactness, the sentences crumble.

> Sexually impulsive patients are *predisposed* to an *infantile regression* because of a *fixation* of a *highly* anaclitic need in relation to a mothering object. *Associated with* such a *primitive* relationship are a *poor* differentiation between the self and the object, an *insufficient neutralization* of libidinal and aggressive impulses, a *persevering operation* of the primal processes of introjection and projection, and a *polymorphous perverse predisposition.* The anaclitic fixation and the association characteristics become *partially* or *completely* separated from the *remaining* ego, a phenomenon similar to Freud's (1919) conception of the genetic construction of the perversions. (italics added)

The author completes this labor with "a postulation" (Is that the scientific term for "a postulate"?) related to "the characteristics described above." But the "postulation" drawn from the quote is unmanageable because so many of its key ideas are beyond the reach of observation, much less of testing. How does one handle such statements? How can we determine what the author means and then test the correctness of the ideas? Citing authorities is, of course, no test; colleagues' nodding their heads is no test; accusing skeptics of being resistant is no test; clinical anecdotes that do not reveal what actually was said and experienced in analysis are not tests. (See also Ellman and Moskowitz, 1980, on reification, giving an abstract noun, e.g., "reason", a name to make it appear a thing; Esman, 1979, on the confusion between evidence and inference; Slap and Levine, 1978, on hybrid conceptions in psychoanalysis.)

The language of science, when experts communicate together, seems esoteric, often incomprehensible, to an untrained observer. But somewhere one can find stipulative definitions for most of that vocabulary. That is not true with analysis. There is scarcely a technical term about which, even today, fundamental disagreements are not elaborated in our literature: the ego, the unconscious, neutralization, cathexis, narcissism, identification, libido, sublimation. And what are the *demonstrable* differences (except that they appeared in different eras) among these words: infantile, pregenital, preoedipal, oral, narcissistic, archaic, or selfobject?

An author writes: "The persistence of a primitive ego component deprives the remaining ego of a considerable amount of energy and thus interferes with the ego's full development." The experienced analyst in me sees what the author means, and, hardly hesitating in my reading, I mobilize my clinical/theory experience sufficiently and move on to the next sentence without despair. But if, instead, I concentrate on my concern with the definitions of our psychoanalytic vocabulary, the sentence turns to gas.

Being mostly a clinician, I am of course forever dissatisfied at not understanding well enough and not being a good enough therapist. So I want help: tell me what actually occurs in the treatment whence you drew your ideas, so that words such as these comes to life: persistence, primitive, ego, component, deprives, remaining, considerable, amount, energy, interferes, full, development. I cannot translate these words into precise, tangible clinical data; that, doctor, is your responsibility. And it is not just that one sentence, for that sentence is embedded in a whole paper written in the same style. And the paper is part of an issue of a journal that is part of a volume that is part of a series that is part of the literature, a literature swollen with that kind of communicating. Phallic prostheses.

> She always took something (a corsage, a napkin, a book of matches) from each boy to put into her file. It must be something concrete, like the hair, which analysis had shown represented her mother's pubic hair and hidden penis, the baby, her father's penis, and her little brother's penis.

Maybe analysis showed that, but the author did not.

> The hypotheses I shall put forward, which relate to very early stages of development, are derived by inference from material gained in the analyses of adults and children, and some of these hypotheses seem to tally with observations familiar in psychiatric work. To substantiate my contentions would require an accumulation of detailed case material for which there is no room in the frame of this paper [There! That's true.] and I hope in further contributions to fill this gap.

She never did; no analyst has.

I wish I could drive psychoanalytic colleagues crazy with such quotes so that they could never again use this stuff comfortably. (I have analyst friends who think they are stupid because they cannot read the kinds of papers from which these quotes come.)

Tentative phrases—"I would say,"; "I think,"; "I hold that,"; "seems to,"; "seems to me,"; "tends to,"; "appears to,"; "may imply some,"; "I suggest that,"; "may be extremely important"—are mixed with flat declarations—"the early ego splits the object," "the faeces nearly always represented a baby and were connected with a passive homosexual attitude to the father". In this way, the rape of my mind is made to seem a seduction.

A related technique: quote a revered authority and thus stake a claim to proof.

> Projection, as we know from Freud, originates from the deflection of the Death Instinct outwards and in my view helps the ego in overcoming anxiety by ridding it of danger and badness.

We know that Freud ruminated, guessed, speculated, and in time became convinced—all, necessarily, without data that adhered to the thesis—that the Death Instinct idea was the true case. We sophisticate like theologians.

> We often fail to realize how far our field has developed and come in the 75 years since Freud's "Interpretation of Dreams" burst on an unreceptive world. [See Sulloway, 1979, for evidence that softens the claims of the world's unreceptiveness.] The range of phenomena, the hypotheses and understanding of mental functioning that have grown in these years is truly impressive. Much that was controversial and uncertain in the early decades of the century have [sic] been widely validated and accepted with new findings built upon them.

Ponder this:

> Due to its archaic structure, the ego is extremely vulnerable to the impact of libidinal stimulation. Renunciation of primitive gratification with original objects becomes impossible. The homosexual's inability to bind the original instinctual energies and to transform them into a potential tonic energy available for secondary process has been cited by Freud. A primitive ego utilizes incorporation to a high degree; the original objects, never really given up, are incorporated into the ego and remain the prototypes of future object choice. However, these objects become incorporated according to their original highly ambivalent cathexis. This contributes to a split and to the ego being filled with contradictory contents. To compound the situation, the weakness of the immature ego does not allow for its synthesis of the originally conflicting attitudes. Here according to Bychowski the analogy to the psychotic or prepsychotic ego is apparent. As a result of this split, the ego may function at times with one or another of its segments, that is, assume the role of one or another of the introjects.

In other words, homosexuals are no damn good. Why can't they behave like normal men, who—we all know . . . no question about it . . . it has been shown over and over—bind the original instinctual energies far better (0.87 vs. 0.19, $p = .001$).

If a scientist's data depend on his writing style (Schwaber, 1976, pp. 516–517), how dependable are his data? Here is an ad that reminds us that Freud needed his power as a writer to overcome the absence of *reportable* data:

7
Our-Science:
The Observing-Instrument

S : *We know; Everyone knows.* What then are we to make of such "data"? At this point, believing it to be a classy defense of psychoanalysis, the scientifically inclined psychoanalyst turns for protection to astronomy (see Rubinstein [1980] for a way to reveal that ploy), or quantum mechanics and its principle of indeterminancy, or to our awareness that data are only interpretations. Oh, yes; but a potato is not a tomato, and when we give a patient an interpretation, we do not feel that anything that could be said is as accurate as what we say. Quite the opposite. We argue like Bishops at a Council, insisting that certain truths are too powerful to question or prove.

Enough of the hokum that because hunches and intuitions can pop out of unconscious depths in anyone, a psychoanalyst is as much a scientist as, say, a chemist dreaming up his benzene ring. "The imaginative sweep of a set of ideas does not confer factual validity upon them" (La Barre, 1980, p. 120).

Here is a hypothesis that I manifest as a suspicion; it should be written in the faintest ink. Every psychoanalyst has thought it, but it goes unsaid: at the bottom of some (how much?) seriously considered analytic theory is poor observation. Supervisors of students in analytic training may feel they have a general idea of the quality of a candidate, but the most careful presentation of clinical work cannot tell the supervisor exactly what happened. (It is not necessary, of course, for the function of the supervision is not to create a science but to help make the student a therapist.) What if the physicist said, "I have discovered the top quark but cannot show you the technology used nor the results. Just believe me"? What if a naturalist tells you, "Crocodiles cry", but you have no way to see his crocodiles?

Most analysts are physicians; we know, from our eight years of undergraduate and medical school courses, what science is. Until the wriggling starts, we connected science with scientific method. Everyone knows that when Freud used "our science", he was trying to link analysis with the natural sciences (viz. Freud's phylogenics); I doubt if he would have happily placed it in the same category as "cards," "writing," or "sport." The Ph.D. analysts also know what the intellectual world means by "science." We are trying to get a free ride when we blather about our-science.

What other science, respected by analysts, does not use some or all of the following interventions as part of its scientific method: testable hypotheses, theory models, the challenging of parts of theory by formal experiments, calibrating its instruments, measurements, organizing data with statistics, using observable/confirmable data, presenting repeatable data, producing new facts, and prediction? What kind of a science is it that has no trusted way to move from guess to validation or as in artillery or golf, from longs and shorts to hits and holes?

Analysts beg dispensation from the rules others accept for defining science, working from the premise that the road to heaven is paved with good intentions. Good intentions: know thyself; end innocence. But not all that ends innocence is science, is it? "By reason of its exclusive ambition to gain explanatory power, psychoanalysis is solidly anchored [the ambition to do well is a solid anchor?] within the scientific tradition." Why say "scientific tradition?" I am suspicious and worry when someone picks phrases like "scientific tradition;" I like to think it shows the author's awareness that he does not feel quite right using the word "science."

> In addition to its love for truth and rationality, science demands detachment, disinterestedness, and hard work. It must be without pettiness and open to everyone. It cannot countenance dogma or reliance on authority but has to use intelligence and curiosity to test hypotheses against evidence. Knowledge must be accumulated with prudence and humility, i.e., with continuing skepticism about the finality of answers. Beyond all this, psychoanalysis espouses honesty, concern for others, and a positive commitment to life and its satisfactions, i.e., a reduction of pain. It encourages sobriety and faithfulness, patience and thoroughness, search and rigor, elegance and precision, moral courage and self-discipline.

We should all agree with this as an ideal for analysis, but because it includes "open to everyone" and "test hypotheses against evidence" in the description but not the practice, we ought not .equate science and psychoanalysis. At the least, the stupefying use of quotes from authorities indicates that psychoanalytic (like canonical and talmudic) scholars operate from a different meaning of "evidence" than is fitting for a scientist.

In real sciences when a rule or finding has been tested and repeatedly confirmed, as Colby says, there is no need—except in a historical study—to credit the discoverer; the discovery has become common knowledge. (When, from here on, I say "real science", "true science", or "genuine science", I am suggesting that, in order to avoid confusing those we address, psychoanalysts restrict the use of "science" to its being a synonym for "scientific method", as that term is defined in the dictionary.) But in analysis, we cite back for generations with only a few of our ideas so acceptable that we do not need "Freud said". Psychoanalysts act as if a field becomes a science by promise and proclamation rather than demonstration.

If, as some say, certain analytic propositions can only be tested on the couch, then analysis is not much of a science. We cannot (at least we have not done so yet) validate any of our theories in the clinical situation. And if not there, then where? How can our field be a science if no concept, word, theory, or idea is definitely ruled out except by being shouted down or anathematized? Why the tendency to splits and cults? Because there is no accepted technique, in the way there is in true sciences, for practitioners to agree on "yes" or "no." (Though consensus is no proof, either, of course.) Nagel's point is pretty well known by now to analysts: "A theory must not be formulated in such a manner that it can always be construed and manipulated so as to explain whatever the actual facts are, no matter whether controlled observation shows one state of affairs to obtain or its opposite" (1959, p. 55). Collins (1980, p. 432) reminds us of "the . . . problem of psychoanalysis as a scientific method in which interpretations had the status of experimental hypotheses that had somehow to be tested without contamination by an experimenter whose prestige was intimately involved in their credibility."

In analytic treatment, we can never say something one way, observe the effects, and then go back to the same situation and give a different response, thereby creating an experiment. To report what happened to colleagues and then ask their opinion of what should have happened next is also no experiment. To record what happened and then replay it to get their opinions would only demonstrate that each colleague interprets the clinical moment differently (Dahl, 1974; Dahl et al., 1978; Gill et al., 1968; Seitz, 1966; Stoller and Geertsma, 1963). Even the consensus we believe we have built among ourselves in regard to clinical concepts (such as transference, repression,

unconscious forces) has not carried us much beyond that early stage
of scientific method: naturalistic observation illuminated by, at best,
a brilliant observer.

Yet, the following exemplifies a common belief:

> From one point of view, every psychoanalysis represents [why "repre-
> sents"; why not "is"?] a validating, replicating experiment of previously
> existing findings and theories. To the degree that psychoanalysts have
> been able to report their findings, there is a high level of *consensual
> validation* of findings and general agreement upon the nature of certain
> phenomena occurring within this dyad experiment. There is the
> reservation in scientific validation of this nature, that each psychoana-
> lytic worker may carry a bias toward discovering only those findings
> that have already been reported, and may have overlooked or not
> "seen" other data that may exist. (Joseph, 1975, pp. 10-11)

One—analyst or patient—can be quoted almost accurately. Perhaps
only a word is changed, or an inflection, or the context, and yet the
whole thing is now somehow all wrong. (This must be one reason
why most public figures fear and hate most reporters. Though even
worse can be the accurate, in-context quote.) The meanings and
communications in a process as intimate as an analysis do not occur
through words alone, but, as everyone knows, in nonverbal expressions, most of which are subliminal or deeper. (If a transcript shows
me saying, "Oh, yeah", how can you know what I meant: comfort,
kindness, sarcasm, boredom, comprehension?)

One of Freud's (1959/1925, p. 34) most noted remarks is: "When,
however, I was at last obliged to recognize that these scenes of
[incest] seduction has never taken place, and that they were only
phantasies which my patients had made up or which I myself had
perhaps forced on them, I was for some time completely at a loss."
The great "perhaps." Who (including Freud) doubts he put words in
his patients' mouths? Yet, he says,

> The danger of our leading a patient astray by suggestion, by persuad-
> ing him to accept things which we ourselves believe but which he
> ought not to, has certainly been enormously exaggerated. [Certainly; of
> course.] An analyst would have had to behave very incorrectly [unsci-
> entifically?] before such a misfortune could overtake him; above all, he
> would have to blame himself with not allowing his patients to have
> their say. I can assert without boasting that such an abuse of 'sugges-
> tion' has never occurred in my practice. (Freud, 1964/1923, p. 262)

I simply do not believe Freud here, nor would I believe any other
analyst who said it. (See Klein, 1981, p. 201 for a view of Jung doing
so.)

Juxtapose this remark of Freud's on suggestion with Riviere's quoted on page 11. Freud did not know he used these effects? Everyone in psychoanalytic circles called Freud "The Professor." Who invented the Professor? Who invented Freud? Read Roustang (1982) who shows how Freud politicized analysis, with effects that are organically part of every analytic organization, all analytic research and writing, in the identity of all analysts, and a presence in every analysis; how Freud created and controlled disciples; how he—rather as in a religion or in the patient's transference (i.e. unfreedom) to the analyst—is the One who knows, which leads to working "in a scholarly way according to the laws of echolalia" (p. 60); how everyone but the One who knows can find what must be known only in Him. This defeats psychoanalysis in all its forms. (See also Zimmerman, 1983 and Kernberg, 1986.)

I know I am not the only one who—wittingly and unwittingly and, when it is over, to my dismay (sometimes)—presses gross or subtle forms of my beliefs on patients. "The patient soon came to sense my conviction that . . ." (Freud, 1955/1918, p. 33). What has happened here to Freud's knowledge of countertransference or blind spots the results of one's culture/era, *weltanschauung*, morality, choice of analytic school, or the state of one's bridgework? To what extent is a treatment hour influenced by previous hours with patients that day? How often do we acknowledge that theories came out of depressed, flamboyant, charismatic, mad, patient, impatient, dull, perverse, borderline, narcissistic, optimistic psychoanalysts whose age, sex, marital mood, financial state, research interests, emphysema, and borborygmi may shape those theories? When I take notes, does the patient think the pencil's scratching means I think the associations are important?

Freud's paper (1937/1964) from which the aforementioned quote on suggestion is taken, "Constructions in Analysis", concerns an issue central to the status of psychoanalysis as science: How accurate are the analyst's interpretations and reconstructions of the psychic and material facts of the patient's past, especially the earliest months. I find Freud's answers in this paper disingenuous. The next is better (Rothstein, 1980, p. 14).

"Biographical truth," Freud wrote to Arnold Zweig, "is not to be had." The truth of a life, he seemed to imply, would always slip away under the biographer's gaze, for where is such truth embodied and how is it confirmed? It can hardly be captured by cataloguing the meals eaten, the homes inhabited, the beliefs and constructions of the intellect, or the reports from colleagues, friends, passers-by. Moreover, the biographer is bound up in the truth he finds. Freud warned Zweig against writing an account of his life: "Anyone turning biographer commits himself to lies, to concealment, to hypocrisy, to flattery, and even to hiding his own lack of understanding". In his own biographical essay on Leonardo da Vinci (a "fiction", he called it) he writes, "Biographers are fixated on their heroes in a quite special way". [This, of course, includes autobiographers.] They idealize or degrade—not only their subject but themselves. The biography, Freud implied elsewhere, may contain all the conflicts and confusions of an analytic session.

But all psychoanalyses are [auto]biographies, and all analytic clinical reports are biographies. Is biography science?

Though not sufficient for defining a science, in the fields commonly accepted as science, colleagues share a massive consensus about what to consider facts, and a large, *shared* technical vocabulary stands behind the descriptions of the events—demonstrable and repeatable—observed. This sharing is voluntary, not coerced, for a consensus also exists regarding the freedom to disagree and the methods to be applied so that new knowledge, which will overthrow old positions, can be acquired. In the practice of real science, the heavy hand of authority and the drawing up of by-laws for the forced observance of faith is minimal. Some will argue with this view (maybe in the future, when great breakthroughs reveal that present-day science was more captive than we could sense), but they ought to see what goes on in psychoanalysis.

In a real science, participants agree—consensibility and consensuality—on huge masses of their observations. They agree about so much that only at the outer edges do they work on disagreement. Though the unknown is immanent in any fact, one does not, in real science, come on it as quickly as in, for example, religion (which is intoxicated by the unknown) or psychoanalysis. For instance, in setting up an experiment to test an idea in quantum mechanics, colleagues share in the mathematics they use, the laws of physics that contribute to the stupendous amount—centuries' worth—of technology today at hand, and the preliminary observations that, because of decades of successful experiments, can now be the ambience in which one searches for aberrant behaviors. But that does not hold for psychoanalytic investigation, where, if two or more analysts try to share, they may not even agree that they have witnessed the same thing or understood their supposedly shared technical language (e.g. the meaning of "narcissism" or the criteria for borderline personality). Analysts pride themselves on consensual validation, but that agreement is often not a shared clinical reality but *an agreement to agree* (and even then only in public), without the sharing having occurred: We really do not know to what extent we have seen and heard the same thing from our patients, because so much of our sharing comes from reading colleagues' *reports*. My main function herein is to demonstrate that our reports—written or spoken—are edited beyond the reach of repeatable observation and of consensual validation.

Except for subject matter, how does the process of communicating one's observations in analysis differ from art criticism? Would we say: "The science of painting"? Or of theology? Or of politics, history, economics? Someone somewhere does. Each time I describe a clinical moment, I leave out essential data. (If you will practice what I preach, you ask here: "Essential to what?")

But analysts never reach the point in their descriptions at which the question of reliability arises, for their descriptions are vague, the terms badly defined, and the data at the mercy of the fierce editing processes (e.g. countertransference, the restrictions of language) that transform experience into communication. It is monstrous of analysts to claim that analysis is a science. We do not even report what *we* do—experience—and how that has influenced what the patient experiences. ("Following my interpretation, the patient understood that . . ."). Let Freud's statement that he never in his practice abused suggestion exemplify the endless times when we must accept a declaration because, as different from genuine science, the data are not available. Instead of observations, there is a fight in which one side argues that, for instance, Freud can be taken at his word because he is Freud while the other argues that he cannot. But all the reasons mobilized cannot tell us what happened in his office.

> Psychoanalytic treatment *is* the basic method of psychoanalytic research. As clinical research, at bedrock it is the method of the expert observer and judge. *The reliability of the research depends upon the reliability of the analysis* . . . The controls on this are better within psychoanalysis than any other treatment method, because of the extensive personal analysis of the analyst, the rigor of his training, and his continuing self-analysis. In addition, the method of supervisory consultations can be used as a control if uncertainty exists." ([my italics except "is"], Lustman, 1963, p. 63)

Who believes this?

Can an accurate report of an analytic treatment be presented? Of course not. Analysis is a process. Yet it must appear in the literature as if it were mostly episodes of understood dreams, salient interpretations, obstacles overcome, accurate reconstructions, and resulting moments of insight and relief, softened by understandings that such reports cannot reproduce the realities of the treatment. The actualities, such as the working through that keeps us at it for years, are beyond the reach of even the best writers. How do you put those hard slow years into a sentence or two, as journal space and readers' patience require?

Take a sentence, any sentence. Imagine it spoken by a particular person. Now by another. And another. And another. Each utterance is different, though the words are the same with each speaker. How, then, are we to know what was said—what was meant—when we read a report of conversation? Only a fine writer can do that and even then only because, in truth, he/she is the puppeteer and the personae his creation. But if one's motive in writing is to reproduce a real conversation, then what shall we do?

When I write, I would like to be better, but cannot, at communicating my version of clinical reality. Yet we could sit down together and, in talking, do it. Talking and writing, we know, are two different languages. To write clearly, one cannot use the same words or syntax as when talking. Direct translation from clinic to paper is impossible. And then, when one writes for an audience, exactness is lost also in the need to keep the reader's attention. We readers are spoiled; we rarely stick to it unless entertained.

What about my different moods as I write? These can shift from hour to hour. Those who do write for publication know it sometimes takes courage to persist in the face of one's certainty that the present words are rubbish. Or a flash of mania can turn a modest phrase into music (or silliness). What about the days when I remember how trivial it is to fuss over the exact meaning of words and that writing is a defense against dreadful avoided realities out there? The reader while reading is subject to the same influences.

What about the slow tides of intellectual and scientific fashions; of belief systems about religion, art, morality; and of aesthetic convictions on proper styles of presentation? All these, at work constantly inside us, shift resonances between author and audience.

Which audience: all audiences are imagined (even those really there). As also are all presenters—authors, speakers, whatever. When I write, I imagine an audience and try to be understood; so I say it this way rather than that. But in fact we are, more or less, Rorschach cards for each other, onto which we project our fantasies of the other's form and intent. (There's an example: what percentage of those who read the last sentence—see, I imagine it being read—are familiar with Rorschachs or the mechanism of projection? If I imagined there are only a few, I might change the metaphor.)

I suddenly realize, at this moment of writing, that, when writing,

I am usually subliminally *talking* to an audience, hearing my voice inflecting, pausing, underlining, insisting, growling, chuckling, complaining—in touch with an imagined someone else who is listening and who I am trying to convince. Someone who hears. But what happens when someone reads without listening or when it is not possible to hear? So I try to invent a written language that reads as if spoken and try—with words, punctuation, placement of words, paragraphing, etc.—to approximate with printed language what musical notation does for music. Then, years later, on re-reading, I find that a sentence that had seemed to be boiled down to one unequivocal meaning is obviously either unclear or could mean something unintended.

All analysts know these points, and yet, I think, many ignore them. In the first place, the number of events—observed clearly, subliminally, unconsciously, or completely missed—in any analytic moment, not to say hour, is immense. Which do we notice and why during the treatment? Which do we remember and how? Freud (1964/1933, p. 159) talks of "the intellectual working-over of carefully scrutinized observations." Exactly there is the problem: Who does the intellectual working over; and just what are carefully scrutinized observations? That word "carefully" in a real science is synonymous with the scientific method. What does "carefully" mean in psychoanalysis?

Which observations do we select for presenting our thesis? Even the audience we choose changes the report: a friend; a seminar; a local, national or international meeting; as a paper to be published in Journal X rather than Journal Y or in a book. What modifications will editors require as the manuscript moves toward publication? Even the machine into which I dictate notes after a treatment hour is an audience—a number of audiences, e.g. I at a later time or people I imagine reading a report. And that "I" is more than one: I, the listener two years from Tuesday; I, the author of a paper; I as my own editor/protector/saboteur. The kind of dictating is drudgery for me. Why? Because the damn machine is my conscience, which I must not only obey but rebel against. (Both take integrity, but the end product is a shift in the notes from what would appear were there no conflict.)

A patient says, "Hello" or "My clothes feel tight" or "I hate you." What is the relationship between the spoken moment and now, when I report it here for you? If one's purpose is scientific, are the differences trivial? How do we know?

So, since we cannot present accurate—and therefore any—data, we must rely on performance to convince others in both our written and spoken presentations, the word "science" being the most stirring sign of legitimacy. "In psychoanalysis, a field unsure of its successes, dependent on the uncertainties of human interaction and misunderstanding, and immersed in the investigation of madness, the value to its practitioners of an assurance that one is practicing science cannot be underestimated [sic]" (Steele, 1979, p. 407).

THE MEASURING INSTRUMENT

Observation, we know, is a process of information-gathering, performed by an instrument. It is impossible to understand the observations unless we can measure the physical form of the observing instrument, the functions built into that form, and the state of the instrument at the instant of observing.

> Psychoanalytic knowledge occupies a special position in relation to other scientific disciplines, because the whole person of the investigator is implicated in the investigation. It is true that the narcissism of any scientist can play tricks on him; but the exact sciences do not require the experimenter to elucidate his personal experience and feelings: in psychoanalysis, on the contrary, the "psychic apparatus" of the psychoanalyst is actually used as an instrument of investigation. (Chiland, 1980, p. 359)

Or:

> The analyst is the measuring instrument in the analytic situation and like any good measuring tool the analyst must be free from distortion. A precondition for the analysand coming to self-understanding is that the analyst must have come to a psychoanalytic self-understanding. The analyst "may not tolerate any resistances in himself . . .", resistances create distortions and hence the recommendation that all analysts "should have undergone a psycho-analytic purification . . ." through a self-analysis or preferably a training analysis (Freud . . .). By 1937 this recommendation is stronger: every analyst must undergo a training analysis; he should use this analysis as the basis for continuing self-analysis; and because his analytic work, in its preoccupation with repressed material, will create distortion in him. "Every analyst should periodically—at intervals of five years or so—submit himself to an analysis once more . . ." (Freud . . .). This makes the analyst's analysis interminable and commits him to an ongoing process of self-reflection in order to gain greater self-understanding. Without such understanding he is incapable of practicing psychoanalysis, for he is incapable of being a reliable psychoanalytic measuring instrument. According to

Habermas (1981) "Psychoanalysis is . . . the only tangible example of a science incorporating methodical self-reflection . . .". A picture is forming of the interlocking circles of interpretation, understanding, and self-reflection required for analytic understanding to be achieved. The analysand's self-understanding is dependent upon the analyst's self-understanding and the analyst is always either the analysand of himself or another analyst. (Steele, 1979, p. 397. See also Gill and Brenman, 1947, p. 216-217; Shakow, 1960; Wallerstein and Sampson, 1971)

Or:

Unless, or until he has been analyzed himself, the would-be psycho-analyst will tend to distort what he hears by ignoring some aspects of it and overemphasizing others. Only a personal analysis, we have learned, offers reasonable assurance that this tendency will be kept to a minimum. (Brenner, 1968, pp. 690-691)

But we analysts know, as we look each other over, that "psycho-analytic purification" is rare; will you base your science on it (Balter et al., 1980)? Perhaps the next great event in the history of analysis will be the emergence of an analyst who reveals himself or herself fully, so that the era of calibrating the measuring instrument can begin (Spence, 1981). It could be as great an adventure as was Freud's—and more dangerous. Guess which group would be the first to attack this crazy exhibitionist?

There are bad reasons (bad science plus bad motives) as well as good (e.g. confidentiality, not revealing publicly our own inner states lest patients' transference reactions be muddied) for our failure to report what goes on in us at a moment of observation. Nonetheless, never once in the history of psychoanalysis—never once—has that instrument been described so that we would know, at the moment of observation, its nature, its form, and its state.

And beyond that, how much of our intrapsychic analyzing activity is beyond our reach? Psychoanalysts are, properly, more and more concerned, for instance, how countertransference (the doctor's neu-rotic reactions to the patient) changes treatment, but there is scarcely a word—Devereux (1967) goes almost unremarked in the analytic literature—how it transforms the process of observation as the fundament (as Freud tells us) of our-science. In a real science, the researcher's personality plays its part; so the greatest effort, perhaps, in scientific methodology is that aimed to reduce the effect of the (particular, idiosyncratic) experimenter on the experiment. It is never zero, but God knows it is less, at the time the experiment unfolds, than happens in psychoanalytic treatment. We would not want the psychoanalyst to be constant as a caliper, but we should face the awareness that our almost infinitely complex sensitivity as instruments of treatment puts us beyond measure as reliable instruments of observation (Baudry, 1982).

OUR HERMENEUTIC SCIENCE

What does it mean that when analysts talk of "our science", the phrase is embedded in a philosophic discourse – in an essay, and not during the presentation of data or new findings?

Because of the way analytic reports are written, we cannot tell how analytic treatment goes about affecting patients, why it works, and why it does not. Yet, who begs that we correct the situation of vague reporting? We are *never* told what was communicated, and almost never what words the analyst and patient said to each other. Analysts' formal reports (publications, presentations at meetings) may contain brilliant, imaginative, unexpected, ingenious, creative, striking insights . . . but, we know, our colleagues and friendly, neutral, or inimical others are often untouched, unconvinced. Because of oral envy? Anal rage? Deneutralized cathexis? Narcissism, primary or secondary? Libidinal synaesthesia? How about bad theory, mistaken observation, little consensus, little trust in the reports, our failure to make clear ideas clear to others and to report clear findings clearly?

What is science for a Kleinian or Lacanian or Bionian is Dada to a nonbeliever. If analysis is a science, its practitioners scientists, and its practice constructed of scientific acts, whence comes the unending process of the splitting off of cultic schools? Or non-cultic splits? Other physicians, for instance, have intense disagreements, but no one doubts that an argument about, for instance, the proper drug for diabetes will be resolved without Medicine fragmenting into naturopathy, chiropractic, osteopathy, homeopathy, or Christian Science. In analysis, one can be a Jungian, then a Freudian, then a Kleinian, and then a Kohutian, and none of the shifts needs be based on new observations, much less protected by scientific method. If you, an analyst, disagree with an interpretation presented in one of our scientific publications, can you show you are right and our colleague wrong? Any analyst who has analyzed or supervised another analyst can measure the discrepancy between public and private reports.

What are the perceived differences between a patient who is "quiet" and one who is "silent"? The decibels in the room are the same, but in the silence is an anger or despair not present in quietness. Yet what the analyst does (which might include being quiet or silent) depends on how that clinical moment is read. Which reading is correct? What are the criteria for "correctness?" Every psychoanalytic moment requires such judgments. Where does our-science begin? Not in the room where the observations are made. (Let me interrupt this polemic for a sentence and hint at short-comings in cognitive science: How will cognitive science deal with these modes of communication, and the ways people disguise their communication, and with noise that has the appearance but not substance of communication?)

The stuff of psychoanalytic work is fantasies, that is, meanings, scenarios, desires, (and "fantasies" includes, to the analyst, more than the conscious scripts we call daydreams) just as food is of cooking and clay of potting. Perhaps we can understand an individual fantasy and think through a theory about fantasizing, but a *science* of fantasies? Though they exist, fantasies cannot be observed, measured, or reproduced. What, then, will be the method of this science and what will be its purpose? Fantasy is not a subject that will submit easily to computational psychology. (I am not now asking what is the method and the purpose of psychoanalysis, for the term "psychoanalysis" means more than the study of "fantasy".) What does "science" consist of in the phrase "the science of hermeneutics"? Will someone allege that "science" is synonymous with "understanding" or "effort to understand"? (Yes; the dictionary.) No one would propose seriously that the *practice* of analysis—the source of the data that are the foundation of the theory and major premises of analysis—is science. Could one say that improvising on a musical instrument is science? Every moment is unique, though there is an underlying structure made of moods, notes, emphases, and rhythms.

The reason there are as many interpretations of a play of Shakespeare's as there are interpreters is that (happily) he could not present the data. (We do not even know what he was trying to evoke.) This tells us that though we all have before us the transcript of what everyone said, we still do not know. So we have a pretty good reason for not fully sharing Gill and Hoffman's (1982) enthusiasm for transcripts as the technique to save psychoanalysis as science. Art is ambiguity. It is a different form of discovery from science (though the two meet where the unknown begins). If critics cannot agree on their interpretations of the plays, where at least the written script may be constant, how can analysts do so regarding a living person in an analytic hour?

Our competitor is the artist, not the true scientist. Art, like analysis, is a dialogue; there is very little dialogue between observer and observed in the true sciences (until one gets to quantum mechanics [Radnitzky in Steele, 1979; Braginski et al., 1980]).

I repeat: If the clinical descriptions in our literature are not accurate, where is our science? I simply do not recognize as humans the teratomas displayed in most psychoanalytic writings. To analyze is to lyse, to dissolve, to break a whole into its component parts. But in trying, as in the literature, to be scientific, descriptions start with the parts already fragmented, macerated, brutalized; our authors do not let us experience the person. The reality of people is wiped out by our authors' desire to be scientific. Let us say that a function of science is to make something clearer—more precise, better understood—and to keep on, forever if necessary, with this process that makes the thing clearer. Though in theory that might be enough activity for defining a science, in practice we have to fill the definition with a second phrase: ". . . and to communicate the findings to others" (to anyone, not just a co-conspirator).

I pick a quote because it appeared on my desk today: Ten thousand others could as well be chosen from any year's analytic literature. "He [Kohut] puts the 'self' into the center of our being from which all initiative springs and where all experience ends". That certainly sounds good; I think about it and measure my experience against it. My argument is not that I do not sense the idea in it but whether ideas like this can represent anything scientific. Sentences at this level of metaphor and abstraction make up the substance of our science; subtract them and a lot of that substance melts away. (Read Leites [1971] and see what is left when he renders the fat off "identity.") So now, instead of just accepting—intuitively understanding—what was written, let us pick at it.

What does that mean: to put the self into the center of our being? Is "our being" different from "the self"; how? What does the metaphor "center of our being" mean; how would you measure a quality that was a bit off that center? What are the realities summarized in "initiative"; remove "initiative" from "the self" and what is the remainder called? What is, in this sense, "experience"; what is "all experience"; what that is observable and measurable occurs "where all experience ends"? How are we to imagine this metaphoric place, this psychic state where all experience ends? What is experience if not perceptions of, in, by—which preposition is correct?—"the self"? How could there be "the self" without there being "initiative" or "experiences"; what would an experience-less self look like? Initiative is energetic; is it then synonymous with "cathexis" or "synthesis" or "energy" or what? (Elsewhere I read of "specific disturbances in the realm of the self." Putting aside my not knowing the rules for distinguishing specific from nonspecific disturbances, I wonder where is the realm of the self and who rules it—the self?)

Now, imagine that you feel you understand these words. Do not just insist to us that you do and that we all share this knowledge, but try to write explicit answers to my questions. In the all-too-sharply-constricted language that writing is (as compared to the arm-flailing, eye-crackling, sea-complex mass of communications that come with speech), the failure of these words would quickly appear.

Is Melanie Klein part of our science? Jung? Horney? Stekel? Reich? Reik? Adler? Bion? Hartmann? Kohut? Freud? The author of the recently reviewed book—or any in the last seventy years—whose work the critic said was "not psychoanalysis?" We know that in the eyes of some legitimate authority (in addition to our own conscience), each of us is not *really* an analyst, only an approximation. In this way, then, there are *no* proven analysts, only psychoanalytic psychotherapists (in the disparaging sense of that label). What real science has to endure that bitter gall: How many chemists claim that co-workers are not only wrong but not chemists?

8

Our-Science:
The Tests Analysts Offer

S : Speaking of the scientific aspects of analysis, one should really also speak of the analyst as a scientist (Hartmann, 1964/1958, p. 317).

Psychoanalysis is scientific and not merely speculative because it has an investigative procedure, the method of free association, which must proceed according to certain rules and contains within in the possibility of testing hypotheses (Levine, 1980, p. 15).

The triumphs of physical science have given "science" an aura of mystical omnipotence, so that all research wishes to claim "scientific status." Rapidly developing or new specialities—anthropology, ethology, sociology, archeology, economics, psychology—all claim to be "science" . . . uncertainty arises as to what is "science." What is the criterion? We might say "science" (from Latin *scio*, to know [sic]) simply means "knowledge." Wherever reliable knowledge is come by, that is science. But what is "knowledge?" (Guntrip, 1978, p. 207.) [And why did that word 'reliable' slip in?]

The hypothesis we have adopted of a psychical apparatus extended in space, expediently put together, developed by the exigencies of life, which give rise to the phenomena of consciousness only at one particular point and under certain conditions—this hypothesis has put us in a position to establish psychology on foundations similar to those of any other science, such, for instance, as physics. [Which foundations? "Similar" in what ways? And how do those foundations differ? I would like to see described the foundations analysis and physics share; and Freud answers:]

93

In our science as in the others the problem is the same: Behind the attributes (qualities) of the object under examination, which are presented directly to our perception, we have to discover something else that is more independent of the particular receptive capacity of our sense organs and that approximates more closely to what may be supposed to be the real state of affairs. We have no hope of being able to reach the latter itself, because it is evident that everything new that we have inferred must nevertheless be translated back into the language of our perceptions, from which it is simply impossible for us to free ourselves (Freud, 1964/1940, p. 196). [Does not the religious believer say the same?]

Psycho-analysis is a scientific method based on what survives of our belief in magical effects (Reik, 1933, p. 321).

Psychoanalytic propositions fulfill the general requirements of theory in science. They unify special assumptions under more general ones, indicate which tests for validation and refutation of specific hypotheses are meaningful, and facilitate the formulation of new hypotheses which in turn can be tested (Kris, 1952, p. 13).

I wish to argue that psychoanalysis is a science rather than a mythology, a "pseudo-science" or a form of religious or aesthetic speculation. The question of the scientific status of psychoanalysis is not of course a new one, but I will argue that recent advances in the philosophy of science have rendered obsolete most previous attempts to answer it (Will, 1980, p. 20).

Kohut and Wolf (1978): "Once the self has crystallized in the interplay of inherited and environmental factors, it aims towards the realization of its own specific programme of action . . .". This clearly represents a whole new scientific paradigm (Chessick, 1980, p. 472). [Why do these authors say "*scientific* paradigm"? And why does the writer who quotes them say "clearly represents" rather than "represents"?]
Etc.
To prove analysis is a science, then, one declares that it is.

THE TERMS "SCIENCE" AND "RESEARCH"

One has to keep in mind that, though related, the terms "science" (when implying scientific method) and "research" are not synonymous; Though there is agreement on the criteria for scientific method, research has broader connotations. Even when we agree not to use "research" as the word for just any organized or scholarly work (such as a library search for authoritative sources), it usually implies keeping records and an effort at discovery. So, for instance, naturalistic observation, though it precedes confirmation, replication, prediction, controls, measurement, and statistics, is research. Darwin was a naturalist, Freud too; but observing, I think, is not yet science (and to repeat—ad nauseam—observations no one else can ever observe cannot be the basis of a true science). Systematic observing—mensuration and quantification—is immensely important early in (the work for which I would restrict the word) science, but for me is not synonymous with science.

I want to be clear, therefore, that for all its uncertainties and occasional bad practices, I believe, from my experience, analytic treatment can be a powerful tool for observing mental functioning, and can lead to new data, new concepts, and new explanations. Yet I am so uneasy on seeing the term "research" used for most of what is called psychoanalytic research, I have scratched it out when describing my work.

I have left out of this discussion the interesting but peripheral issue of research that is about analytic concepts but not about analytic (therapeutic) technique and its reliability as a research tool. Much of that formal research is shaped by awareness of scientific method, but most of it, as Hartmann (1964/1958, p. 317) said has "not so far decisively contributed toward a reformulation of psychoanalytic theory." (Perhaps that is because, as Hartmann believes, the research is trivial. And perhaps also, analytic theory is impervious to correction by research.)

INTERPRETATION, RECONSTRUCTION, QUANTIFICATION, AND "THE TRUE ESSENCE OF THE ANALYTIC EVENT"

Waelder (1962) wrote more carefully than most on the issue of psychoanalysis as science. He makes the point that philosophers, in contrast to practitioners of science (such as physicists), discredit analysis because it does not have adequate tools for quantification. A misreading of what I am saying would make me seem to be on the side of those philosophers, but I am not. I have not said that analysis needs techniques for quantifying in order to do its work—treatment and discovery—but that it needs methods of quantifying if it wishes to insist it is a science (i.e., a field committed to scientific method—a syllogism, because a necessary part of scientific method is quantification). Nowhere have I said—simply because I do not believe it—that, as some philosophers (e.g., Hook, 1959) say, analysis is a pretty worthless endeavor for studying the mind. I am only insisting that *our nervous complacency in declaring we do science helps us avoid doing better work.* (And, perhaps, other discoveries we might make if our morale were not low because we energetically keep denying the weakness of this our-science of ours.) Psychoanalysis is investigation, sometimes research. Not all fruitful investigation requires scientific method. (Freud's *Project* and Chapter VII of *The Interpretation of Dreams* have been the models for our-science; they have been marvelously seductive and would as well serve us as warnings.)

Analysts (Freud too?), are, embarrassed that analysis—practice, theory, data, research tool—is weak, but our telling ourselves we are scientists is immodest and unnecessary. The task we have taken on—to understand mental processes—is tough, and our failure so far to clarify issues as well as did, say Newton and Einstein, need not make us defensive. "It is very difficult, perhaps impossible", Waelder (1962, p. 116) reminds us, "to prove by mere outside evidence even so simple a statement as this: John is deeply in love with Mary. It is desperately difficult to find clear criteria to distinguish deep love from more shallow relationships, or from make-believe, or self-deception. But is it really necessary? Are introspection and empathy not sources of information too, *not infallible*, to be sure, but *not negligible* either?" Waelder goes on:

> As analysis proceeds, mistaken interpretations will gradually wither away, inaccurate or incomplete interpretations will be amended or completed, and emotional prejudices of the patient will gradually be overcome. (p. 629)

Oh, yes? Can we be sure? How do we come to trust Waelder's propositions? By the patient's improvement? By our own sense of conviction? In fact, I believe Waelder's statement is correct, having sometimes experienced the process. But how does it happen and how often? If analysts could answer that and lay open the observations they used so others could also judge, we might build ourselves a science.

We can use a recent paper by Spence (1981) as a response to Waelder's ideas. Spence begins at the center of my pain:

The current dissatisfaction with psychoanalytic treatment and theory—
what some have called a crisis of confidence—raises the issue of
whether we practice what we preach. To what extent does the
psychoanalytic literature convey what we do? To what extent does our
literature function, as in other professions, as a mode of communication, and to what extent does it operate as a kind of projective screen,
peopled by each analyst with his private set of patients? To what extent
does our psychoanalytic training make us particularly blind to this
danger and tempted to overlook the fact that much of the time we
neither accurately represent our clinical experience nor adequately
understand the experience of others? (p. 113)

Spence, like others, writes of our dependence on "the analysing
instrument" and how the analyst is not a *tabula rasa* when listening to
the patient (p. 113). In doing so, Spence also distinguishes between
the analyst's "normative competence", the competence (knowledge)
we all share, for example, as a result of our training and common
literature and "privileged competence", the complex comprehension
of the particular patient only the treating analyst can have:

> We see here a contrast with literary competence which is presumed to
> be sufficient for the understanding of literary texts; no privileged
> information about the author is assumed to be necessary except in
> certain special cases.

> By contrast, normative psychoanalytic competence, although neces-
> sary, is probably never sufficient for even a moderate degree of clinical
> understanding; not even privileged competence always suffices! (p.
> 114)

Therefore, we can never understand the clinical moment that lies
behind a report without "the private commentaries of the analyst" (p.
114), because no one else understands the full context.

Spence then quotes Culler:

> To naturalize a text is to bring it into relation with a type of discourse
> or model which is already, in some sense, natural and legible . . . To
> naturalize . . . is to make the text intelligible by relating it to various
> models of coherence. (p. 115)

In other words, to edit until intelligible. It follows, then, that there
is *no way* that the clinical moment can ever be recaptured by an
audience bent on science. Too much goes on, and too much of that is
forever invisible, hidden in the skull.

Spence and I differ (as I do with Wallerstein, 1971) in that Spence accepts, as accurate enough, the narrative produced by "naturalizing a text":

> A narrative explanation becomes convincing by virtue of how many details of the case it includes, and the way in which the details are presented . . . only when the treating analyst has fully naturalized the text will it become equally understandable and convincing to the reader with normative competence. (p. 115)

But there we have the old problem; is it accurate because it is convincing? How full is "fully"?

I do not see where we go from here. In my own work, I have hit the wall at this point: publishing extended narratives with "naturalized texts". Over the years, I have become frantic with the failure of our literature to be convincing when presenting lines of argument and, along with a few others, have tried to do better by presenting more direct quotations and by "naturalizing" to increase the reader's view of what went on inside patients and myself. I have been successful, at least to the extent of convincing myself that these presentations of clinical data are truer than most I read. I also enlarged the technique by having the patients, in the two books that each took up one case, read and correct the entire text. But many distortions remain; one cannot compress years of treatment and innumerable issues into even a piece as expansive as a book: It would take many books to "naturalize the text" of a five minute exchange between two people.

Emotions are hard to portray with printed words. We cannot bang drums or fire cannons to indicate hearts beating. That does not mean we cannot *stir* emotions; any pornographer can do that. But it takes skill to convey, by writing, what a character felt, so that the reader also feels it (which is more than the reader just being told what the character felt). In other words, a good psychoanalytic report requires talent, and a great one requires art. And art is fiction. Its intent may be to tell the truth, but its technique is invention. [C: Psychoanalysis is to science as metallurgy is to chemistry. S: Colby is being uncommonly kind now.] So I think it is impossible: the more accurate we try to make our reports, the more they fail unless we add our own narrative. And that brings us back to the writer's subjectivity.

As if the problems were not awful enough, Spence notes (p. 117) what we all know, that the longer we pause before writing up our impressions of the hour, the more those impressions either fade or begin leaning to one side of accuracy or the other. Freud's admonition not to take notes is important, but his waiting till late at night to write up his patients did not improve his science. When I dictate process notes into the machine immediately after an hour (usually, however, I wait till later in the day), the material has already begun to shift, to fade, to tug at me to forget it. But who is to say which would be the truer version: the one dictated immediately after the hour, or two hours, or later that day, or the next day? And is dictation better than writing by hand?

Spence says, "To avoid . . . misreadings, the private feelings of the treating analyst (and his reflections on them) must be added to the record—and they must be added before too much time has passed, before they no longer are available" (p. 117). As the years passed, I came to do this more and more, but in doing so, I now realize there is no end. Describing our inner experiences during a treatment hour could fill as many books as could the narrative on what the patient said, felt, and meant. Once again, the whole truth is impossible, even if one were both motivated and competent to try for it. For there is no whole truth. A final selection from Spence who condemns, but not enough:

> What, then, is our literature? With only a few prominent exceptions it does not contain the true essence of the analytic event because the treating analyst as author does not see the need to supply confirming evidence and therefore does not naturalize the material sufficiently to make it available to his colleague. (p. 122)

To me, the situation is even worse. Spence has assumed that there is, somewhere, "the true essence of the analytic event." But that is wrong. Who is the God or reliable machine, fixed in time, place, and person, who is the Absolute against which we can make our measurements? Only It knows the true essence of the analytic event.

At the heart of our-science is interpretation, explaining the hidden meaning of manifestations. The most spectacular interpretations are reconstructions of the past, back through the years to childhood, to infancy, to birth, and, in some circles, to the alleged complex mental activities of the fetus, perhaps even (in the deepest reaches of Kleinian Brazil and Scientology) to cognitions at the moment of conception. Heady stuff, astonishments of our-science perhaps more marvelous than even the astrophysicists'.

But how shall we receive these announcements, beyond test, beyond argument? For infants cannot talk or otherwise turn to machinery of communication that would externalize the content of their alleged fantasies. Because one can never find confirming or disconfirming observations, I suggest a simple shrug of the shoulder, (which, I believe, is as effective in these futile circumstances as is scholarship and carefully honed argument, especially if one is busy).

Steele and Jacobsen (1978) have done the careful work necessary to show how much of analytic reconstruction is, starting with Freud, soggy ground on which to build a science. Using repeated examples of Freud's reconstructing, they show his claims for the validity of his descriptions of unseen events from the patient's distant past to be shot through with speculations and rhetorical devices—"Freud's theoretical manoeuverings" (p. 402), "familiar Freudian tactics of theorizing" (p. 403). They look, for instance, at Freud's insisting that "[The Wolfman's] seduction is certainly not a fantasy" and point out the absence of direct evidence, the use of assertions that are not facts, arbitrary exclusion of other equally logical explanations, enthusiastic acceptance of selected patient reports if they fit a theory, and other defensive maneuvers mobilized to preserve *a priori* positions. (See also Mahony, 1986.)

We cannot validate an interpretation (though we convince ourselves, e.g. by the manner of the patient's response or by the agreement of colleagues). Direct observation of the past is impossible (and analysts almost never make use of even meager confirmatory evidence such as snapshots, home movies, letters, or corroboration from relatives.) Where, then, is the similarity between analysis and the accepted sciences? Well, you say, how do we confirm reconstructions such as the big-bang cosmologic theory: Theories are, by definition, logical but inadequately tested explanations. So I shrug and limit myself to asking you: granting the similarities, what are the differences between the astrophysicist's theories of genesis and those of a Fundamentalist pastor? And which is likely to shift, given new data or theory?

Discussing the origin of Freud's theories on sexuality, Jacobsen and Steele (1979) note:

> Freud says that the material for this work was synthesized from three sources: (1) direct observation of children, (2) the conscious memories of adult neurotics in psychoanalytic treatment, and (3) 'from the inferences and constructions, and from the unconscious memories translated into conscious material, which result from the psychoanalysis of neurotics' . . . In the essay Freud does not clearly distinguish which of the three sources a specific sexual theory comes from. Although such a measure would be methodologically desirable, for Freud it is unnecessary. He is, as he says, providing a 'synthesis' from the three sources. For him reconstructions of the adult past that provide information of childhood are equivalent to the actual thoughts and behaviours of children. (p. 353)

Most of us would agree that accepting adults' reports of childhood in place of observations of children can cause trouble. And how are we to continue a discussion with Freud if he rejects counter-arguments because, as he threatens, they "would place us outside psycho-analysis"?

Analytic reconstructions, in the treatment situation, can be facilitating without that happy result being proof of the reconstruction's validity. It is also obvious that, without recourse to evidence collected outside the analytic situation, and without better confirmation than the patient's agreement (or disagreement) a reconstruction is also not validated. No natural science has such rules of evidence. If one wants to look into the heart of our-science (reconstruction) read Jacobsen and Steele (1979, pp. 353-358). There, we see that Freud's method of science is a synthesis of meager observations and massive, arbitrary, and idiosyncratic speculations quite beyond the reach of proof. Has there ever been a psychoanalytic interpretation/reconstruction where another would not also fit? And this is the stew from which our-science emerges.

DATA COLLECTING IN THE CLINICAL SITUATION

In analytic treatment, moment by moment with the patient, I side with those who go by what is resonating in us, set off by the patient. If we are fortunate/skillful, what we feel is induced not only by ourself but reproduces (now, in our own style) what is going on in the patient. (Our response should not be called countertransference, though as with everything else that can ever happen to us, it partakes of our past life. Those who call all of the therapist's responses countertransference do us no favors, for their terminology does not distinguish what is crucial in treatment—that we can tell the difference between what is primarily our problem and what is primarily the patient's. If everything, equally, is countertransference, then how shall we ever know what goes on in the patient or whether what we feel the patient does to us *is* what the patient does to us? Where, then, is empathy? And if what we hear from the patient is just our distortion, how can we interpret the patient's responses?)

What else can we do in the clinical situation, if we are to be constantly in touch with the patient, other than fly by the seat of our pants? Our-science has not progressed beyond the era of barnstorming. Unfortunately, some analysts' pants should not be flown by the seat of, either because their own neurosis (countertransference) prevents their resonating or because they may not be (independent of countertransference) any good. At any rate, all I have to go on is my capacity to reproduce in myself my patient's interior at that moment; hardly a scientific technology.

In the treatment, I am not a mirror—most everyone now feels Freud used a poor metaphor there—but a musical instrument that is to resonate when played. The playing consists of the innumerable conscious, liminal, and subliminal motions with which the patient moves me, some of which are meant to be communications and some of which are, from the patient's point of view, epiphenomena. If this is our first meeting, I can factor only the grosser impressions, but with time I am not even conscious of most of what I perceive in order to understand what goes on in the patient. In this regard, much of the communicating is beyond words.

We know that understanding others comes not only from the words used but also from the dense mass of microscopic signals that give meaning to the words. (The absence of that information in text makes it, except in skilled hands, an ambiguous way to present motivated behavior. And with an artist, as noted above, that ambiguity is desired because it reproduces much of the reality of humans relating.) When we do this subliminal observing correctly, our patients think we read their minds, though we are simply listening with our bodies (Reik's Third Ear). Quite literally, our bodies.

We use this process, more or less, with everyone, not just while analyzing: Meaning/interpretation is everything everywhere. So, the fundamental process of the practice of analysis (and therefore the data collecting in analysis) is "intuition"—empathy, resonance—*not* the scientific method. (This is not to say that empathy is enough—the only tool—for analytic practice, only that it is indispensable for and the ground from which arises the work of interpretation.) I shall cater here to those who demand it and say that I know this creative, intuitive process is necessary for science and that any piece of work, such as an experiment, that is not enlivened by these internal processes is either uninspired rock-grinding data-collecting or worthless.

This wide-open-to-anything listening (for those good at it) is keenly sensitive. It handles the unmeasurable bytes of information in an instant but is not reducible to mathematical or experimental study. It is fallible, idiosyncratic, genuinely unscientific. Yet—I repeat and repeat and repeat—there are no other psychoanalysis-derived data supporting psychoanalytic theory.

Suppose it turned out that only good clinicians collected reliable data? (Granting how hard it is to judge the quality of data since they emerge only after passing through the observer's enigmatizing mind. No neutral machine, like an ohmmeter, gives the report.) How would anyone know? Suppose some of the trouble with analysis is that we have no scales for differentiating the useful from the junk? How can we ever know when a brilliant theory is based on lousy practice? (Not that invalid data necessarily invalidate theory.) We are so far from being scientific that we haven't the faintest idea on what data any of our theories are based. Therefore, we have no way to test our theories. How often have others told us that?

In these circumstances it may come to pass that the most respected people are the thick tongued, neologizing grand thinkers. They tend to be unenthusiastic about details, which are so untidy. But without the seat of your pants—whatever the thrills and risks—you think and interpret by means of theory, jargon, hot tips from colleagues, advertisements (note the spoilage of valued concepts, such as self, transitional object, separation-individuation), and artless imitation of others.

WHAT CRITERIA ARE USED TO INCLUDE PSYCHOANALYSIS IN SCIENCE?

Most analysts have believed that analysis is a science, but, in any case other than analysis, they are as uninterested as I am in opening up the definition of "science" so wide that it includes the fields accepted by the dictionary. "Basic scientific methods must be the same for all the sciences" (Kaplan, 1981, p. 4). What are the qualities basic to analysts when arguing that psychoanalysis is science?

Creative imagination (underlying both slow, careful work and epiphany), search for information, search for truth, ingenuity, research, originality, discovering, "rendering intelligible the phenomena of the world" (Will, 1980, p. 204), capacity to reason, belief in determinism, focal optimism (i.e. "grim hope" [Collins, 1980, p. 429]), attraction to integrity, constructing models of the phenomena to be understood, "repetition of configurations" (Modell, 1978, p. 170), search for and formulation of general principles (Breger, 1981, p. 36–37) in order to find "law, order and connection" (Freud, 1955 [1913], p. 174), unique data (Brenner, 1980, pp. 205-206), sublimated curiosity, desire to understand nature (including the mental processes commonly called mind), a method of investigation, a search for insight into processes, concern with "asserting true propositions about reality" (Edelson, 1977, p. 2), desire to discover the laws hidden in the manifest, "proclaiming our ignorance" (Pollock, 1980, p. 6), appreciation of the natural sciences from biology to physics, courage, commitment, rational thinking (even in examining the irrational), and (perhaps) eccentricity.

Fine attributes achievable by analysts and legitimate aspects of science. Where, then, is the problem? I find it exemplified in this next belief.

> . . . however different are the data of psychoanalysis from the data of other [!] natural sciences, its method is the same: observation and accumulation of data by the best available method(s) that is (are) suited to the purpose. On the basis of the data thus accumulated, one generalizes as best one can and tests one's generalizations as rigorously as possible after they have been formulated. The method of psychoanalysis is not introspection . . . nor is it the drawing of logically sound conclusions from assumptions established a priori. It is the method of natural science applied to the data of psychology. (Brenner, 1980, p. 207)

The problem lies behind the brave words "best available method(s)" and "test's one's generalizations as rigorously as possible." Because the best available methods of analysis fail tests by any standard of testing—we can never review the findings—the claim is unjustified. If we are left only with intentions such as those above, analysis would not be much more science than are astrology, alchemy, chiromancy, phrenology, or theology.

Bacon's "skepticism about the efficacy of medicine" in his day holds for psychoanalysis today: "a science which hath been more professed than laboured, and more laboured than advanced" (Stone, 1981, p. 36). Of course, I do not feel it is as hopeless to argue about premises in analysis as, say, in a religion, astrology, or quack medicine. I am an analyst because analysis is a workable tool for looking at people and worry about our-science because analysts really have—pardon the expression—a scientific conscience, at bottom not corrupted. I cannot believe that analysts, in the quiet of their souls, are not aware of the trashiness of our theory and clinical reports that my quotes herein indicate.

> In sum: psychoanalysis is *not* a science, but it shares some of the qualities associated with a scientific approach—the search for truth, understanding, honesty, openness to the import of the observation and evidence, and a skeptical stance toward authority. (Breger, 1981, p. 50)

How then shall I talk of analysis? Colby suggests "heuristic", which the dictionary (Webster's 1961) defines as "Serving to guide, discover, or reveal; *specif*: valuable for stimulating or conducting empirical research but unproved or incapable of proof—often used of arguments, methods, or constructs that assume or postulate what remains to be proven or that lead a person to find for himself".

END

Our our-science problems start with Freud, of course. His fine intellect and his medical training showed him the power of scientific method, and yet, despite his embarrassment and disavowals, he could not contain his impulses toward philosophy. How could he, if he was to move from studying the brain to studying the mind? Presumably, those of us most attracted to Freud's work bring to it those same two themes.

At any rate, the struggle to be scientific has been perpetuated in analysts to the present. Freud's daydream of analysis as a force in the world of science still haunts us. From his family to his followers, products of his ambition—the scientistic metapsychology; the vocabulary of science used for patching weak arguments; the premature announcements of success in solving great biologic problems (such as the function of dreams, psychic energy as the power that drives behavior, instinct theories, humoral theories of neuroses [e.g. damming of libido])—have been supported more than his ideals. (The ideal I like most is his skepticism.)

How did so many intelligent and decent people perpetuate the mess exemplified in these earlier pages? Mainly by hero-worship, that antithesis of science: "Freud said . . .", "Freud himself . . ." (that same "himself" used for Boston-Irish political bosses). When prepared by education and experience, one can easily spend each day with Freud, learning, arguing, pondering, ruminating. He is, for most analysts, well beyond anyone else psychology ever produced. We are regularly astonished. But why the worship? That is a whole other category than respect: we need worship only if we cannot doubt well. (Sulloway, 1979, handles, with high scholarship, these issues of the falsehoods inherent in hero-worship.)

Freud was not a hero. He discovered nothing because he was a hero; he did not work hard because he was a hero; he did not suffer quietly because he was a hero; he did not persist stubbornly because he was a hero. Heroes do what they do because they are heroes, like being able to quack because you are a duck. Hero-worship denies his achievements, makes him god-oid. It is shot through with dishonesty, never quite cut free from its connections with flattery, self-deception, megalomania through contiguity, and its lust for ambivalence. (It's partly Freud's fault, though. He was a hero-worshipper. And hero-worshippers spawn hero-worshippers, Roustang, 1982.)

Is Freud so vulnerable, so open to being compromised that an official line must be created and maintained for him? I think of the club for conquistadors he was so happy to have secretly arranged for him. Is that heroic band and their fraternity rings of ancient design admirable? When Freud talks of his "splended isolation" and proud stance in the face of being either ignored or getting bad reviews ("like a glorious heroic age"), look at Decker's careful search of the journals and magazines of the time (1977) that shows that he was not at all ignored and that even those who disagreed with him acknowledged that his work was powerful, provocative, and original?

Freud, the hero-worshipper, has created a movement of hero-worshippers, of cult creators (though at the same time he condemned such behavior). How can that action not produce apostles, with their hidden rebellions?

Analysts conspire with the most childish of Freud's fantasies to produce Our Freud. The headline for a New York Times Book Review asks, "Did Freud Have Clay Feet?" That is, was Freud human? That such a crazy question can be headlined is Freud's doing, and his friends, his family, his colleagues, and analysts from then to now. When we are done fooling ourselves, we shall loosen our demand on Freud and accept that he comes from the clay that forms us all. To pretend otherwise—to censor the truth—is one more oedipal myth, the opposite of all that analysis stands for.

I bet physicists do not idolize their best people. If fully involved in their work and fully committed to themselves as physicists—I innocently imagine—they admire, respect, honor, and emulate but with the clear eye that lets one also disagree and move on. Physics is not a good ground for mythifying or creating mysteries.

We should look closely at what Freud says about *anything,* clinical or theoretical. But that is not because he has science to buttress his remarks. Rather, we listen because he is smart, creative, original, provocative, articulate, informed, occasionally modest (when the moment is important enough to him), committed, experienced, well-motivated, a truth-seeker, and because so many of his ideas, when we use them, seem (if clinical) confirmed, and (if theoretical) enlarge our view of the clinical. He allows us, if you release him from the imprisonment of idolatry, to ask our own questions and to see better the importance of his questions. It would be too bad to spoil that.

Our ambitions overreach our abilities. But that is not the end of it. Compared to others (ethnographers and sociologists, for instance) who also rely on data gathered from people talking together, the analyst has fine skills, whereas many of the others, in their ignorance and their ignoring the complexities of the mind and of two minds interrelating, often have neither wit nor talent to know what they do not know. We analysts have nothing to teach our friends (and ourselves) about science, but we do about the perils of naivete in the clinical situation, the power of the researcher's self-deceptions, the value of listening well, and the gifts that trust provides.

Because Freud created our our-science, it may be too clever to quote him in arguing that we cannot yet say analysis is science. I do so anyway; for if we stay modest and recognize how flawed we are scientifically, we shall try harder. Then some day our descendants (should there be any) will know what we have no right yet to declare, that ours was a proto, not a pseudo, science, "an attempt by responsible enquirers to establish a new branch of science" (Kennedy, 1959, p. 272).

We have often heard it maintained that sciences should be built up on clear and sharply defined basic concepts. In actual fact no science, not even the most exact, begins with such definitions. The true beginning of scientific activity consists rather in describing phenomena and then in proceeding to group, classify and correlate them. Even at the stage of description it is not possible to avoid applying certain abstract ideas to the material in hand, ideas derived from somewhere or other but certainly not from the new observations alone. Such ideas—which will later become the basis concepts of the science—are still more indispensable as the material is further worked over. They must at first necessarily possess some degree of indefiniteness; there can be no question of any clear delimitation of their content. So long as they remain in this condition, we come to an understanding about their meaning by making repeated references to the material of observation from which they appear to have been derived, but upon which, in fact, they have been imposed. Thus, strictly speaking, they are in the nature of conventions—although everything depends on their not being arbitrarily chosen but determined by their having significant relations to the empirical material, relations that we seem to sense before we can clearly recognize and demonstrate them. It is only after more thorough investigation of the field of observation that we are able to formulate its basic scientific concepts with increased precision, and progressively so to modify them that they become serviceable and consistent over a wide area. Then, indeed, the time may have come to confine them in definitions. The advance of knowledge, however, does not tolerate any rigidity even in definitions. Physics furnishes an excellent illustration of the way in which even "basic concepts" that have been established in the form of definitions are constantly being altered in their content. (Freud, 1957 [1915], p. 117)

So we are not a science. It could be worse.

This discussion of Our-Science is, then, the contribution of the clinician, a demonstration that psychoanalytic theories are not based on good report but on rhetoric. There is an immense weight—the vast, now ninety-years-long psychoanalytic literature—on the side of the scales that holds psychoanalysis as the heroic science. So, I have chosen not to counterbalance those bloated writings with only a few and meager quotations easily brushed aside as misrepresentations, but instead have plopped onto our side of the scale a goodly portion of gross, undigestible slabs of fat carved from that literature.

That done, we return to Colby's effort to point toward non-rhetorical, manipulable, reproducible ways of modeling the mind.

9

Folk Psychology

C: Folk psychology is naive, common sense psychology. (Which folk? Whose common sense? Dostoevsky's folk psychology is not that of our man on the street.) It contains aphorisms, mottos, maxims, platitudes, tenacious truisms, maxims, superstitions, and warnings. It tries to explain, for example, why drivers stop at a red traffic light: they stop because they believe if they don't stop they will get run over or get a ticket; or they believe it is the right thing to do; or it is so automatic they don't consciously think about it. Commonsense psychology attributes beliefs, feelings, desires, plans, expectations, and intentional actions to people.

Folk psychology is getting a lot of attention these days from philosophers interested in cognitive science (Dennett, 1981, 1987; Fodor, 1980; 1987; Stitch, 1983). And deservedly so. The errors and absurdities of folk physics and folk medicine can be brushed aside in our enlightened times, but it is not so easy to completely dismiss folk psychology. Why not? Aren't its beliefs as misguided as those of folk physics, in which, for example, many people still believe that an object released from a flying airplane will fall straight down? Commonsense folk psychology contains many similar misconceptions. Why shouldn't we just dismiss it? Why should cognitive science pay so much attention to it? It is because naive folk psychology, despite its shortcomings, is packed with information and predictive power indispensable in the conduct of everyday life and having no available alternative "scientific" theories to rival it in this regard. We use commonsense psychology to explain ourselves to ourselves. This is not an argument for reliability but for indispensability (Fodor, 1987). The main problem of folk psychology is that it lacks a systematic inquiry procedure, a research agenda. Folk wisdom is secure but irresponsible, whereas scientific knowledge is responsible but insecure.

Folk psychology addresses important issues. The major problems of human life involve the cooperation, competition, and conflicts of human relations. A scientific psychology cannot completely ignore the constraints of obviously effective maxims and truisms of human relations. To be valued as a serious contribution to human flourishing, it must satisfy some of the commonplace generalizations of naive psychology that are patently successful in the conduct of everyday life. Many of its platitudes can be safely abandoned. Scientific theories will not completely jettison folk psychology truisms, such as "People have expectations," because these are phenomena deserving explanation. Rival theories may offer different mechanisms for explaining such crude regularities. In a computational theory of mind, the mechanisms involved are described in terms whose meanings may be unfamiliar to ordinary language, for example, recursive list structures or NLAMBDA functions. Commonsense psychology, which we acquire to a large extent from natural language, provides explananda in everyday terms; the underlying explanatory mechanisms proposed by cognitive science are described in the language of a computational theory of mind.

Folk psychology confounds the linguistic expression of content — a partial and gross approximation — with the psychosemantic content of the underlying encoded construals. But this folk explanandum puts *some* constraints on the theories that satisfy them. Also naive psychology evolves over time and becomes enriched by scientific knowledge just as the literate person now believes that the earth moves, in contrast to his belief a few centuries ago. Concepts of information processing and computers are already part of educated commonsense psychology.

Folk psychology offers facts, empirical generalizations, and theoretical explanations.

FACTS

Facts about people and their artifacts are astoundingly dependable if one stops to think about the myriad of details of daily life. Counting on commonsense knowledge, we put our life on the line every time we enter highway traffic. The stock of facts is full of muddles and mistakes, but predictions based on folk facts often turn out to be accurate. If a hundred people from all over the world agree to attend a scientific conference in Paris on a particular date at a particular time, one can safely predict that many will do so.

Besides being reliable, the facts are diverse. Ordinary language has thousands of natural-kind terms. We know thousands and perhaps hundreds of thousands of facts about people and artifacts. As travel and communication increase, more facts are stored as the data of commonsense knowledge.

The weakness of folk psychology facts is their poor coherence. Folk facts constitute a catalog, not a system. They are not systematically connected. I could tell you many facts about where I live—the town has two gas stations, the main road runs east and west, there is a bank on the corner. These facts are all true, but they would not help you find where I live. You need a map or directions connecting them to get to where I live. Folk psychology appeals to beliefs, desires, and feelings, but it is silent on how these entities are organized and ordered to produce unfolding sequences of actions.

EMPIRICAL GENERALIZATIONS

"Men are aggressive. . . . Women are passive. . . ." Such folk generalizations are weak because they have so many exceptions. They are cited as maxims in conversation, but as generalizations they are poor guides to action in specific cases.

Commonsense generalizations are often inconsistent. "Men are better than women at athletic activities. Women are better than men at aerobic exercising." Such contradictions make the generalizations difficult to systematize.

> *The problem is to discriminate exactly what we know vaguely.*
>
> —Whitehead

Vagueness is an annoying (but often useful) property of folk psychologic generalizations. "Add a pinch of salt," where a pinch can vary widely. In practical actions of everyday life, this vagueness is reduced by context.

Generalizations vary in coverage. To say "Each member X of kind K thus far examined has property P" proposes a low-level generalization based on a sample of one or more individuals. To assert "Any member X of kind K is likely to have property P" (without stating the degree of likelihood) is the next strongest generalization. A universal, exceptionless, lawlike statement would read "Every member X of kind K has property P." In the cognitive sciences, it is the "each" and "any" level (accompanied by a degree of likelihood) that is aspired to. Many folk generalizations fail to reach this level of dependability.

THEORETICAL EXPLANATION

Folk psychology might seem far removed from what is called theory in systematic inquiry. Yet the explanatory entities appealed to (desire, belief, expectation) are unobservable and are simply hypothesized in intentionalistic explanation. "Every time a brush fire approaches their house, the Colbys evaculate to a beach because they believe the house may burn down. They desire not to be burned; so they plan to evacuate to a beach." This explanation of the Colbys' actions makes sense of their behavior and predicts accurately. The difficulty with these explanatory entities as they stand is that folk psychology, lacking a systematic research agenda cannot specify their structure nor be precise about their roles in generating actions.

Sellars (1963) proposed that we distinguish the Manifest Image from the Scientific Image. The Manifest Image of appearances is the stories of common sense, whereas the Scientific Image consists of stories provided by the sciences. For example, the temperature of a room in the Manifest Image is a matter of heat. In the Scientific Image, it is a matter of the mean kinetic energy of gas molecules. Sellars did not, however, claim that the Manifest Image is unscientific.

> The contrast I have in mind is not that between an *unscientific* conception of man-in-the-world and a *scientific* one, but between that conception which limits itself to what correlational techniques can tell us about perceptible and introspective events and which postulates imperceptible objects and events for the purpose of explaining correlations among observables. (p. 19)

Thus heat is perceptible, but the kinetic energy of molecules is not. The Scientific Image has prospered because it has been more successful than the Manifest Image in effectiveness, prediction, and control in areas of great significance to human welfare, for example, infectious diseases.

Folk psychology uses imperceptibles (belief, desire, and the like) to explain perceptible action. In that sense it is a naive scientific psychology (Brand, 1984) helpful in pursuing a mature cognitive science. The explanations of folk psychology can in turn be taken as surface explananda, being among those phenomena that a depth-computational psychology tries to explain.

Stitch (1983) claims that theoretical folk entities are not useful for a serious cognitive science. But denaturalized, everyday terms, such as "force" and "charm" are common in the natural sciences. They have been de-naturalized by acquiring special meanings. Words like "belief" and "desire" take on technical meanings in a computational theory of the mind that vindicates much of commonsense psychology as causally explanatory (Fodor, 1987). The entities of the explanatory computational mechanisms of cognitive science may not be *called* "belief", "desire", and the like. Already in computational models the computational equivalent of "belief" is a type of data-structure with property lists (Abelson, 1973; Colby, 1973) and "desire" is represented as a complex tree-structure of goals and subgoals (Mueller, 1987; Schank & Abelson, 1977). These computational entities are specified in programs as much richer structures than the simple labels of folk psychology would indicate. For example, in the language of folk psychology, "desire" is conflated with "intention". "Intention" in computational models is a more intricate composite made up of inferences, affects, goals, and plans to carry out sequences of actions. A problem for computational psychology is how to map the simple typifications and entities of a rumpled folk psychology into the complex, fine-structure composites of computational functions. Such functions in a programming language are no longer easily describable in ordinary folk psychology language.

Generalizations of folk psychology are notoriously weak, superficial, and misleading in dealing with extreme deflections and departures from the ideal. Commonsense psychology falls back on classificatory platitudes to explain a large lapse from the expected. The typifications of folk psychology for deflections—"He's crazy," "She is gay"—are inadequate explanations even at the level of commonsense wisdom. To say that someone is a member of a class is not to state the reasons, causes, or underlying mechanisms that generated the behavior in question.

A major entity of naive psychology is the ubiquitous "I," as in "I believe," "I want". Sometimes the pronoun refers to the whole system, an indexical "I"; sometimes to a subjective sense of "I"; and sometimes to an inner "I" (a homunculus) a theory explaining the whole "I." Since these pronoun assignments are enigmatic in folk psychology, it is difficult to know who or what is being considered as an explanatory device. Cognitive science must attempt to get the story of "I" straight. We now get into that.

10
Homunctionalism

C: A homunculus is a little man or fellow. Here is Paracelsus' (1493-1591) recipe for making one. (It doesn't work.)

> If the sperm, enclosed in a hermetically sealed glass, is buried in horse manure for about forty days and properly magnetized, it begins to live and to move. After such a time it bears the form and resemblance of a human being, but it will be transparent and without a corpus. If it is now artifically fed with the arcanum of human blood until it is about forty weeks old, it will live.

Eighteenth-century microscopists saw a homunculus as a fully formed diminutive human in the head of a spermatozoan. In a roundabout way, the microscopists held a partial truth because what is in the head of a spermatozoan are DNA molecules carrying a program of instructions for building, among other things, a man.

Among the notable homunculi of philosophic thought are Leibniz's Monads. Leibniz (cited in Saw, 1954) concluded:

1. All the beings in the world are of the same kind, and they are more like minds than anything else in our experience.

2. These beings differ from one another in degree; they range from

115

spirits, including human beings, through animals and plants, to "inanimate" objects.

3. They can do nothing to one another, nor can they be said, literally, to know one another. (p. 42)

The term "Monad" emphasizes oneness and simplicity; the plural, "Monads," indicated a multiplicity of them. Monads are the ultimate simple substances, or basic units, of the world, simple in that they have no spatial parts and are infinite in number. They have no "windows through which anything can come in or go out" (Leibniz, 1714), and that they have no effect on one another is obscure. No two Monads are alike, and each reflects (mirrors) the universe from its own viewpoint. For Leibniz, men were colonies of Monads with a dominant Monad being a spirit. (Since it was difficult, even for Bertrand Russell, to get this straight, we have no intention of trying.) Laplace's (1820) homunculus was an omniscient demon:

> Given for one instant an intelligence which could comprehend all the forces by which nature is animated and the respective situation of the beings who compose it—an intelligence sufficiently vast to submit these data to analysis—it would embrace in the same formula the movements of the greatest bodies of the universe and those of the lightest atom; for it nothing would be uncertain and the future, as the past, would be present to its eyes.

It is unclear whether the demon interacted with the universe and irrelevant whether this is Laplace's description of an idealized self. The demon would have a hard time of it nowadays. It could not have continuously and completely updated knowledge of its own states, and thus there would still be room for uncertainty. Also he would be faced with by Gödel's first incompleteness theorem, demonstrating that it is impossible to derive all the consequences of an axiom system. Finally, he would be defeated by the combination of measurement uncertainty of particles, exponential amplifications that lead to random unpredictability even in deterministic systems, and the fact that particles are no longer considered fundamental (it's strings and superstrings nowadays). We are grateful to Laplace for the following: "Human reason has less difficulty in making progress than in investigating itself."

Maxwell's (1868) demon was a 19th-century homunculus used in thermodynamics to relate entropy and statistical probability. This "very small but lively being" could operate a frictionless valve allowing fast-moving molecules, as determined by simple inspection, into one chamber and slow-moving ones into another. His sorting resulted in an order contraverting the law of entropy. What the 20th century decided was that the demon must use energy to operate the valve and the more information he extracts about X, the less he can get about not-X, because the extraction process increases the entropy of not-X. A gain of knowledge in one area involves a sacrifice of knowledge somewhere else, but a lively demon interested only in X might not care what happens in not-X.

Using a metaphor similar to Maxwell's demon, Freud (1917) proposed a doorkeeper or watchman who allowed some mental impulses to pass into a consciousness room and refused entry to others, which then remained unconscious. "Let us therefore compare the system of the unconscious to a large entrance hall in which the mental impulses jostle one another like separate individual. Adjoining this entrance hall is a second, narrower room—a kind of drawing room—in which consciousness, too, resides. But on the threshold between these two rooms a watchman performs his function: he examines different mental impulses, acts as a censor, and will not admit them into the drawing room if they displease him." (p. 295)

Another homuncular system was an interesting visual pattern-recognition program in early artificial intelligence called PANDEMO-NIUM (Selfridge, 1958), which used a lattice of homunculi called demons. Each lower level demon made a decision regarding a feature of a pattern, and each higher level demon made a decision about that decision. Depending on which demon shouted loudest, the topmost demon made a final decision about whether a pattern-type was present.

Many attempts to explain human behavior have postulated that inside a man is another man, for example, a helmsman, inside of whom there is another man, and so on. Since they were doomed to infinitely regress, such explanations were deemed absurd and impossible. (If the mind were infinite, it could contain a model of itself just as the infinite set of integers contains the even integers as an isomorphic group). In current artificial intelligence, it seems that little men are called on to carry out complex mental activities. Consider the following decision box in a flow diagram of a computer model simulating the paranoid mode of thought (Fig. 2).

At the level of implementing the flow-diagram description, how could such a complex decision be made? Easy. Put a little man in the box; a homunculus judges and decides. He must have the ability (and goal) to evaluate the natural language expressions of an interviewer and to judge whether they refer to a network of delusional ideas. Surely such a complex task would require nothing less than a person (probably a psychiatrist) to carry it out. Hence a computational theory

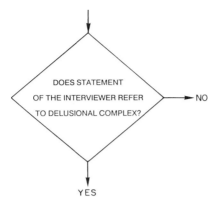

DOES STATEMENT
OF THE INTERVIEWER REFER
TO DELUSIONAL COMPLEX?

NO

YES

Figure 2. A decision box from a flow chart of PARRY.

of mind involving homunculi must be absurd and impossible. But it is not. Functioning homunculi thrive in computational cognitive modeling. "Homunctionalism" is Lycan's (1981, 1987) wonderful term for this perspective.

Those who have written off psychoanalysis as a dead end may be surprised that certain psychoanalytic concepts (for example, unconscious censors) could have heuristic appeal to the computational modeler. Yet they do, for their homuncular nature suit a systematic interpretive analysis at the semantic-representational level (Cummins, 1983). As illustrated by the consciousness doorkeeper referred to earlier, Freud, an eloquent story-teller of stirring narrative powers, tried to explain mental activity with many analogies and metaphors intended to be understood by an educated person at a commonsense level. He used examples from chemistry, botany, crystallography, zoology, and toxicology. His metaphors were economic, military, electromagnetic, sociopolitical, fluid-flow, horse-and-rider. This patchwork of metaphors did not come from obtuse vacillation but from his belief that "what is psychical is something so unique . . . that no one comparison can reflect its nature" (Freud, 1918,). Freud eventually partitioned the mind into homuncular entities (ego, id, superego) charged with the capacities of whole persons: the ego feels itself hated by the superego; the ego attempts to force itself upon the id as a love object; "If the ego has successfully resisted a temptation to do something which would be objectionable to the superego, it feels raised in its self-esteem and strengthened in its pride, as though it had made some precious acquisition" (Freud, 1938, p. 206).

Freud struggled for years to conceptualize mind using a duality of impersonal and personal entities. He proposed first one set of impersonal theories, having what he took to be the elite status of science, and later another set of homuncular theories that reflected his own introspections as well as those of patients describing their troubled subjective experiences. A person's subjective experience of self is that of many "selves," a collective of homuncular persons. (See page 123.)

> *I was not one man only, but the steady parade hour after hour of an army in close formation, in which there appeared, according to the moment, impassioned men, indifferent men, jealous men—jealous men no two of whom were jealous of the same woman.*
>
> —Proust

In the positivistic science of Freud's time, to be scientific was to speak in impersonal terms of particles-in-motion, energies, quantities, forces. To treat mental entities as if they were homunculi was considered to be too anthropomorphic to be scientific. What theorists lacked until recently, when computers came along, was a clear concept of what might be the nature of something lying "between defensive reflex and condemning judgement" (Freud, 1905, p. 175), that is, between properties of purely mechanical systems and mental-processing symbolic properties of goal-pursuing persons.

Multiple metaphors and homunculi in psychoanalytic explanations soon led to conceptual incoherence. Questions of agency and responsibility arose. Who does X? Do *I* sleep? Who is "I"? Do *I* dream? Who's in charge here? The ego turned out to be doing not only the sleeping but also the dreaming. The id was portrayed as a human little rascal, both sexual and murderous, who had to be tamed by a civilizing ego. Instinctual wishes were minipeople striving for freedom against an unconscious, repressing miniperson that itself had to be conscious of what it was repressing and why.

Abstract algorithms realized as computational procedures in programs made up of designed functions are our contemporary homunculi. They are characterized by what they do and are supposed to do, rather than by what physical stuff they are made of. Computational algorithms bridge the gap between the machine ideal of classical mechanism and the anthropomorphism of the total person as unitary agent. Between the physical and the conscious subjective-experiential, we insert further layers and linkages that try to do justice to the physicosymbolic complexity of mental activity in a goal-pursuing mental system. The homunctionalist perspective is subpersonal, not impersonal.

Freud's (1914) belief that "all our provisional ideas in psychology will presumably some day be based on an organic substructure" (p. 78) would today be a truism if "based on" is taken to mean simply physical embodiment, as programs are embodied or realized in computer hardware. Clearly, the concepts and language of physics are not adequate or intended to capture generalizations at the symbolic-semantic level of a goal-pursuing system that simultaneously has symbolic and material properties. Computation certainly depends on hardware devices, but hardware organizational principles will not capture the semantic-structure generalizations of an algorithmic psychology. Freud's homuncular hypotheses may not have been right, but, however crude, they pointed to the right strategy for purposive functional explanation of the mental. Freud, late on (1933a) expressed a notion of what we now term a software-hardware distinction when he stated that anxiety functioned as a warning signal and "what it is made of is unimportant" (p. 85). At the hardware device level, the medium or substrate is physicochemical, to be described in physicochemical terms. At the semantic-representational level, we need a different set of concepts, organizing principles, theory, and vocabulary. The various homunculi of computational talk—algorithms, functions, modules, input analyzers (Fodor, 1983), interrupt programs (Clippinger, 1977), specialists (Minsky, 1986), representors, generators, processors, and sub-processors—are different, however, from the classical little men. They have causal powers because of their physical grounding in hardware; they have directive control powers because of their semantic derivations using computational functions.

Computationalist jargon uses intentionalistic terms of folk psychology, attributing properties of belief, desire, expectation, and the like to running computational models: "It thinks you are not a doctor"; "it wants to insult you"; "it is trying to start an argument" (said about PARRY). These anthropomorphic attributions are convenient abbreviatory devices, intelligible higher level summaries of lower level processes in the computing system. This does not imply that the attributions accurately describe the details of the underlying running processes. We do not yet know the microdetails of what goes on in the mind. Even if we did, we would not have the time to describe the billions of details of microscopic states and events. We would still need higher level, communicable, macroscopic descriptions in terms of overall characterizations and principles. Intentionalistic terminology is useful because it conveys the same type of information to a questioner desiring an explanation of what people of this reference class, whose structure is incompletely known, are doing in similar circumstances.

To describe their running models, algorithmists may talk as if the computational model contain a group of homunculi who encode representations, post messages, perform tasks, farm out jobs, compete with one another, form compromises, bid for control. These homuncular agents are actually computational functions organized into algorithms and specified in a programming language. To stretch an historical association, such homunculi, like Monads, are not all the same in their capacities and details. They are not simply smaller but otherwise exact replicas duplicating the entire repertoire of a total person. They are specialists (Clippinger, 1977; Minsky, 1986). Unlike Monads, they all, from the simplest to the most complex, have the capacity to take in, process, and produce symbolic expressions. They each have procedures for operating on symbols. Like a person, each is a goal-pursuing symbol-processing system. Each is irreducibly purposive and in each, meaningfulness is unremovable. That is, each individual homuncular function at one level can be further decomposed into a group of simpler and more specialized homuncular functions at a subordinate level until the well-known threatened regress is broken in a computing system at the level of known physical-hardware instantiation. Each homunculus, at each level of job-type, performs a specific, irreducible to physics, purposive-symboling function. The tokens (physical shapes) of the simplest homuncular functions still retain meaningfulness because they are symbols. It is an all-or-none principle of meaningfulness that something is a symbol or it is not. If meaningfulness is removed from a physical shape that is about something other than itself, then the physical shape is purely physical, having no symbolic function. A physical shape has some interpretation or it does not.

Functional explanations of computationalism refer to a coalition of homunculi each of whom performs a specific task. Overall molar behavior is the net effect of collaborating and competing individual homunculi that represent differentiated centers of control that bid for dominance. (If the homunculi speak different languages, misunderstandings to the point of conflict can arise.) There is no master homunculus, no one locus of control. (The "I" of conscious experience as a unitary center of control is a subjective illusion.)

I think, therefore I am.

—Descartes

It would be difficult to pack so large a number of errors into so few words.

—Bertrand Russell

Each homuncular agent, from overall algorithm to simplest function, is a specialist (a microperson?) put there by the designer to perform a particular job. And though all homunculi are irreducibly purposive and meaning bearing, they vary in detail, versatility, specialization, and sophistication. Homuncular theory is not doomed to infinite regress (as Dennett thought in 1969 but, refreshingly, admitted the mistake in 1978), because the homunculi become simpler and more specialized, eventually bottoming out in a known physical instantiation having an interpretation. The problem of regress is resolved by the computer analogy. The simplest homunculus is an elementary, symbol-processing system that can semantically answer yes or no to a simple question. At the bottom, at the hardware/device level, such a process is physically instantiated in, for example, a bi-stable switch whose voltage is on or off (Dennett, 1978, pp. 80-81).

Reductionist fears that the mental will be crudely reduced to the physical are unwarranted as the arguments rejecting type-type identities have demonstrated (Fodor, 1975; Pylyshyn, 1984). In a subpersonal computational psychology, the intentional systemic properties of an overall system are explained in terms of organizations of algorithms (differentiated homunculi) composed of computational functions that themselves are goal-pursuing subsystems with purposive systemic properties at the systematic-interpretive level of analysis (Cummins, 1983). A composition relation differs from an identity relation. A whole acquires its properties from a composition of parts, processes, and their organization. Because a system is itself designed (engineered), it does not follow that a systematic study of it is engineering. Such homuncular explanations are, alas, dehumanizing in the sense that the total person is explained in terms of delineated parts. It might be some consolation to those with homunculus horror, however, that properties of some of the parts can still be talked about in a functional language we would use in describing a whole person, for example, having goals, even though goals in the models of computational psychology are composed of designed functions.

11

Homunculosis

S : For this discussion of homunculi, let me stay at the clinician's level, where the experience of subjectivity is described, rather than at Colby's computational level. (The lower levels, we know, do not deny the existence of their surface manifestations any more than quarks indicate that shoes do not exist.)

I speak in praise of homunculi though belief in them is declassé in psychoanalysis today. The effort has value (I especially enjoy Dennett, 1978, for appreciating them), even if antihomuncular psychoanalysts are correct that the little folk of metapsychology—ego, id, superego, the Unconscious—do not exist: These anthropomorphs of classical psychoanalysis do not match subjective reality—what we think, feel, remember, fantasize.

My homunculi are real in the sense that they are experienced, describable. They are the "people"—inner objects, part-objects, object representations, fantasized objects, psychic representations, and identifications are the sorts of names they are given in psychoanalysis—behind the raw material (what everyone thinks, feels, says) from which we build our theories. Homunculi are functions, including desires, presented as scripts: people at work.

In the following examples, each person, including each "I," exists *in me* as a formed, motivated, portrayed person. I get up in the morning and say, "I am not myself today." If mentally ill, I mean that literally: during the night, They invaded my mind with machines and stole me from myself, replacing me with someone else. Usually I mean only that I had too much steak and wine for dinner. Or, I wonder as I write, Who is the audience? What I imagine the audience is determines every word in each sentence. Or, while this present sentence was moving toward consciousness, I remembered a tune

123

from childhood about The Seven Dwarfs (homunculi). Along with the melody and its words came pictures from the movie. The tune, the words, the pictures are homunculi. Or, I remember my father in a particular scene. He, in my remembering, is a homunculus. Every memory of him (and there must be billions, rather like the so-many-frames per second of movement in a movie) is homuncular, each a person, each at least minutely different from all the rest. Or, my conscience, that crowd of moralizers, says, "Don't do that", "Good job." Or, "So I said to myself. . . ." Or, I, the inept joketeller (which is only one piece of me) tell a joke: "There were two Irishmen, Pat and Mike. They were on their way to Dublin when . . . ," wherein Pat and Mike, if the joke is to be told well, must be my familiars. The process psychoanalysts call "identification" is homuncular. Or, "For the good of my cause, I must hijack a plane and shoot passengers. They are evil; I am good. I blast anyone who disagrees"; projecting accusations against ourselves onto others is homuncular. Or, "Colby, you're right. I agree with you." Or, here is the picture of a man dressed in women's lingerie, shamefaced, bullied by beautiful women with whips, a favorite pornography for some transvestites, who, when little, were deeply humiliated when the act depicted in the pornography was done to them in reality. All the characters in the story either exist in the transvestite, or he does not comprehend and so does not become excited. His erotic excitement depends on the homunculi. Or, "I am possessed by the Devil; that is why I did it." Or "I love you and have loved you since the moment I met you." Or, "Last night I dreamed I was in a crowd of people when I was suddenly approached by a man. . . ." Or, "Following my heart transplant, while delirious I experienced a monster of horrible visage ravaging my chest." Or, the night of my first attack of malaria, I dreamed of aborigines firing masses of wire-thin, red, needlelike arrows at me. Or, ". . . the possibility that an idea may exist simultaneously in two places in the mental apparatus" (Freud, 1914). Or, "My fibroids have a mind of their own; for the first time I understand. . . ." Or, "I do not understand why I get turned on by putting soot on a woman's hands but not when I see a woman with already sooty hands." Or (from the first reported dream in the treatment of a woman who in adolescence had wanted to be a nun and whose son dresses in females' clothes):

> There were two of me—an amazing, unpleasant feeling. One was standing facing one way, the other another way—backward. That one was holding a lot of cloth and moving backward toward something dark. It was like a study in perspective in painting, like a dark tunnel.

I felt myself to be the one who was looking at myself – other one, going backwards. The look on that one's face – the one going backwards – was sly. She had taken the cloth.

Or, the patient with multiple personality, who has several selves at the same time. Or, "Yesterday upon the stair, I met a man who wasn't there. He wasn't there again today. Oh how I wish he'd go away." Or, the imposter . . . the actor . . . the playwright . . . the novelist . . . I, myself. Or, I who tell you the dream I had last night, the dream created by an I whom I have never met though he lives in me. Or, looking at oneself in the mirror. Or remembering. "I remember one day when I was five, I . . . ," and that child is still there in me. Or, a daydream, with each of its characters. Or, music. Or, the repressed parts of me that influence my behavior without my knowing they exist. Or, our love objects, perceived by us as living outside us but not loved unless infused with our interior (an interior populated by homunculi). Or, my experience of my internal organs, limbs, skin, ("body ego"). Or, food, drinks, their packages; every thing we anthropomorphize, (which may be everything); pills. Or, the sane person who hides within the insane person, the insightful person within the neurotic. Or, slips of the tongue: Who speaks when we want to be silent? Or, the clock in our head that wakes us at the right instant. Or, the effects of hypnosis. Or, trance . . . conversion reaction (e.g. hysterical paralyses) . . . automatic writing . . . speaking in tongues . . . "identification" in a happy marriage . . . bisexuality. Or, I look at my picture in the family album. Or, "I have a cold"; "I have an itch." Or, theriomorphism, the ascription of animal characteristics to humans ("I am hungry as a bear"). Or, "I don't exist. I'm only the product of my imagination."

Mental life, then, is populated by homunculi, our closest relatives.

Freud tried to avoid the unscientific feel of a language filled with the homunculi of our subjectivity. He disconnected, by writing style, from the populace within us who possess them, the forces of our-science: resistances, excitations, impulses, presences, currents, flows, blockages, drives, energies, states that defend themselves, urges, loci. Consider the following quote. Every psychoanalyst knows that the highest reaches of our our-science are filled with such passages. Would we suffer without such talk? (Note the dwarfs at work.)

The assumption that the ego directs countercathexes against the id is essential to any study of preconscious mental processes; also essential is the assumption that a preconscious process from which the ego

withdraws cathexis becomes subject to cathexis with id (mobile) energy
and will be drawn into the primary process (the basic assumption of the
psychoanalytic theory of dream formation). The reverse (unconscious
material becomes preconscious) occurs when id derivatives are
cathected with ego energy and become part of preconscious mental
processes at a considerable distance from the original impulse. They
may do so if changes in the distribution of countercathexis have taken
place, e.g., if the level of conflict has been reduced and the id impulse
has become more acceptable; also, they may sometimes enter preconscious mental processes at a considerable price in terms of symptoms.
Id contents may also reach consciousness without ever becoming
preconscious. Metaphorically speaking, they may become accessible to
the ego not from within but from without. They then appear as
percepts, acquiring at once, as it were, the hypercathexis required
for consciousness. This is an abnormal (or rare) pathway to consciousness, the pathway of hallucination. We consider it by contrast as
normal when preconscious material reaches consciousness by a further
increase in cathexis, the hypercathexis mediated by attention. In some
cases, however, this hypercathexis cannot become effective without
considerable effort. This is the reason why we assume the working—at
the passage into consciousness—of countercathectic energies that
would prevent what is, to some extent, egodystonic from entering full
awareness. [Kris, 1952, p. 306]

"Ego", "superego", and "id" are poor homunculi because, by not
doing justice to our subjective experience, they lead to sloppy
theorizing. Self psychology, an attempt to improve matters by
returning "self" to psychoanalysis, is for me, mostly weak
homunculation. It cannot even define "self." Is "self" synonymous
with "mind", "soul", "mental", "identity", "personality", "character
structure", "subjectivity"? Described by observable features, not
theory words, how does it differ from "ego"? The experts do not
agree. "Self" can cover over, obscure, ignore the subjectivity of those
it describes, letting the theory that the word "self" carries these days
in our literature do the work.

We also need to beware the self psychologists' use of "self" as an
indivisible subjectivity rather than as the sum of many active parts
synthesized into an illusion of unity we feel (when not psychotic or
when not dreaming). But if psychoanalysis has any assignment, it is
to decompose that utilitarian, necessary sense of intactness into its
components. My thesis is that the subjective experience of those
components takes place in the form of the wee folk, living out their
assigned scripts and trying to influence, push around, or bully other
homunculi. And even if someone comes up with an acceptable

definition of "self", the self would still just be one of the grander homunculi.

The homunculi's problem is, as I imagine it, that they are megalomanic: each, including my "I," thinks it runs its show, if not the whole show. Worse, each thinks it thinks. That is, each thinks *it* creates its thinking. (PARRY is Colby's puppet. Could PARRY be programmed to think he thinks?) Perhaps you know Lem's (1978) wonderful story of the world created by computer programmers. The inhabitants thought they were feeling, three-dimensional people dimly aware that there was a god that had created them. Each believed in its own free will. (I am not sure that they are not at least partly correct.) Perhaps oddest of all in this construction is that few homunculi know to what extent their existence depends on other homunculi or on other factors, for example, somatic or cultural ones, that an outsider would say silently control them. (What a shame my free will is invaded by—worse, depends on—things in me I cannot control, cannot even feel exist.) When I experience myself as spontaneous, to what extent is the spontaneity a lovely illusion?

Which leads to an issue avoided by many cognitive scientists: levels of awareness. Observable (by oneself or others) manifestations of mental processes—thoughts, feelings, desires, fantasies, memories, motivated actions—change, depending on the degree to which the processes are conscious, preconscious, or unconscious. We are, in general, at the mercy of a thought we cannot accept and therefore do not feel. For instance: a flyer amnesic from fearful combat is psychically paralyzed. He is freed when after hypnosis the lost, terrifying memories are recovered. For instance: fear of his homoerotic desires can make a man fanatically heterosexual.

In these examples, the conflicts between the opposing desires to know and to forget are experienced in the subject as scripts: homunculi in purposive action. "I [homunculus] want to eat [purposive action]." If I am dieting, this desire is opposed by "I [another homunculus] shall not want to eat [purposive action]" (that is, "I want to not want"). So, with our fanatic, we have a script like this: "I want; but that is dreadful; therefore I shall not want; and so I do not want. Those who do want are dreadful; they must be punished. The impulse is everywhere [always present in me but denied]; I must be ever-vigilant; so I smite them; which is good. I am good."

To begin the process of modeling the mind, then, we should start at this subjective level, where scripts are displayed and enacted. Because this is folk psychology, not yet scientific, because beneath the simplicity of discovered scripts is complexity, such as unconscious processes and defenses, psychoanalysts, ever since Freud, have turned to headier stuff: grand explanatory theory (the grandest called metapsychology). In this effort, analysts like most scholars of the mind, have been motivated to find the structure—the unities (elements and their relationships)—that underlie the infinite permutations on words and desires that humans can create. In addition, psychoanalytic theory making has been top-heavy in comparison to the flimsy clinical reports from which it is built. Nonetheless desire and the desire to defend against desire may be among the most important problems that psychoanalysts have faced and that other mind modelers have sidestepped or, worse, denied.

The need to know the level of awareness of the homunculi also indicates that whatever their failings psychoanalysts are on the side of the angels in insisting that desire, a multilayered experience, is central to a good model. It may be easier for nonclinicians—academics removed from the interpersonal demands of the treatment situation (especially if they crave pure thought)—to ignore the concept of desire. But there is nothing like psychopathology to focus one's attention on desire.

Once the immediate, manifest states of the mind have been identified and described (naturalistic observation as the first stage in scientific inquiry), then the search for underlying structure/dynamics can proceed. And it is there that the cognitive scientist can move, with theses from psychoanalytic psychology, into stronger explanations of mental functions. The mistake for psychoanalysis, as many have recently noted, was to turn to physicalistic explanations—the flow of energy—rather than to mentalistic explanations—information, communication, interpretation, meaning: homunculi in action. Our perspective here does not preclude psychoanalysis from changing into what most analysts say is its mission of being a science, though it will not look like current psychoanalysis. We also believe that in working on problems of naturalistic observation, psychoanalysts can minimize their cultist propensities.

12

Computational Psychology

A mighty maze! But not without a plan.

—A. Pope

The last thing to be discovered in any science is what the science is really about. Men go on groping for centuries, guided merely by a dim instinct and a puzzled curiosity, till at last some great truth is loosened.

—Whitehead

We don't know where we're going or how we will get there but we know one thing—when we get there we'll be there—which is something even if it's nothing.

—S.J. Perelman

The end is nothing, the road is all.

—W. Cather

C: Computational psychology grew out of computer science and attempts to simulate higher mental functions in the 1950s. The label "artificial intelligence" (proposed by John McCarthy in 1956) was refreshing because it freed the new field from the strictures of an ineffectual psychology and from a computer science devoted mainly to hardware architectures and programs for number-crunching problems. The behavioristic psychology of the time suffered from a huge blind spot in denying mental processes. It scorned the wisdoms of folk psychology and philosophy of mind regarding belief, desire, and meaning. In contrast, artificial intelligence (AI) was interested, not

129

just in "intelligence" but in the more general question of what the mind does and what it potentially can do. AI took commonsense psychology seriously as a starting point. It took the bold step of trying to formulate the more successful entities and explanations of naive commonsense psychology in explanatory computational terms. AI provided a research agenda to explore and check out aspects of commonsense psychology using the methods of computational model construction.

The early intelligence artificers believed that some mental processes (postulated as existents) could be explained in terms of programmable symbolic processes (Newell, 1973). Of necessity (one cannot do everything) they did not address problems of sentience, consciousness, history dependence, adaptive learning, self-intervention, person-to-person understanding, and morality. Subdivisions in the field appeared. Some wished to create smart machines or robots (McCarthy, 1960; Minsky, 1963); some wished to model or simulate human mental processes (Abelson, 1963; Colby, 1963); and some did both (Newell & Simon, 1972; Simon, 1969). Some wanted to help people become smarter and some wanted to help people become better.

The aim of some artificial intelligence work was to get computing systems to perform intelligent tasks in any way possible, without claiming this was the way people did it. Another aim was to simulate mental activities by programming an explanatory theory of how human mental systems actually operated. This aim characterizes computational psychology, which, along with psychology, philosophy, linguistics, artificial intelligence, and neuroscience, contributes to cognitive science. (Whether cognitive science will suffer the failings of the behavioral sciences remains to be seen.) Cognitive science is characterized by the computational theory of mind, in which mental systems are not just described in symbols but viewed as literally consisting of symbols (Newell, 1981).

In building a smart computing system—cognitive engineering—one uses the scientific or rough-and-ready knowledge at hand, regardless of how people are thought to "do it." In modeling aspects of a mind, computational psychology is constrained by the goal of developing principles explaining the way people do it. Cognitive engineering programs, such as expert systems, do not model, for example, affects—processes that a good mental model must include. There are overlaps in the endeavors because in constructing, for instance, a successful chess-playing program, one employs heuristics (king safety, center control) used by successful human chess players. The resulting program, however, is not intended as a model of how people play chess, nor is it based on a theory *explaining* how people play chess. In contrast, in modeling a paranoid mind, the theory, algorithm, and programs involved are intended to illuminate and explain what actually goes on in minds afflicted by paranoid processes (Colby, 1981). Computational psychology is a depth-functional psychology that aims to contribute to cognitive science by creating programmable theories and models such that the phenomena and processes generating them can be made to occur on demand. When a novel object is created, one never knows all its properties. Numbers have been around for a long time, but we still do not know all the properties of these mathematical entities. Likewise for computational models of the mind.

> *The idea is the seed; the method is the earth.*
>
> — C. Barnard

Methods depend on the nature of the inquiry. Traditional psychology in the empiricist tradition has seen its central problem to be collecting and systematizing data. Computational psychology sees the task as developing better idealizing theories and models to explain existing scattered, piecemeal data that have not led to a coherent theory and model of the mind. A well-recognized (but virtuous) circularity arises because empirical observation is driven by idealizing theories that determine what data are relevant. Theories require data both as the explananda and as one means for warranting the theories as adequate or useful.

Systematized data (low-level natural-kind generalizations refined from the singular statements of raw data and brought under the conceptualizations of relevant background knowledge) provide the generalization patterns (empirical invariants) that supply problems for solution. In the pursuit phase of inquiry, these general patterns involve at least a preliminary classification of kinds that must be agreed on for systematic inquiry to get off the ground.

> *The first step in science is to know one thing from another.*
>
> — Linnaeus

> *A dog is an animal recognized by other dogs to be such.*
>
> — Samuel Johnson

> *The discovery and classification of kinds is an early but indispensable stage in the development of systematic knowledge . . . Indeed, the development of comprehensive*

theoretical systems seems to be possible only after a preliminary classification of kinds has been achieved.

—Nagel, (italics added)

The patterns to be explained—sequences of properties of objects or events—are structures in which the "places" in the structure are occupied by interrelated classes, types, categories, or groups described in a language whose terms are consensible, that is, whose competent users agree on meanings so that statements can be used for unambiguous communication. As we have discussed (chapter 4), because psychoanalysis lacks consensibility, its theories have not been empirically warranted. It is not that the clinical reports are uncongenial to psychoanalytic theory but that the "data" offered consist of reportorial fictives as explained in the foregoing chapters.

Computational explanation of observable input/output patterns connects them (makes sense of them, confers intelligibility) by positing an internal structure of effective computational patterns (functions) that unify them into an organized whole. The existence, persistence, and change of the observable data-patterns are accounted for by showing how they are the products of a stringent structure of nonobservable patterns capable of generating many patterns at the observational level of systematized data. Computational explanations are a type of pattern explanation: they appeal to theoretical patterns to explain empirical patterns. They attempt to unify heterogeneous facts that are difficult to connect and make sense of otherwise. Uniting them as generated by an underlying core of computational functions makes intelligible a range of seemingly disparate phenomena. How is all this done? By starting with clear cases having a preliminary taxonomic reliability and building a theoretical system.

THEORIES AND MODELS

Theories are insights which are neither true nor false but, rather, clear in certain domains, and unclear when extended beyond those domains.

—D. Bohm (1980)

A theory should be offered with a smile.

—Szent-Gyorgi

That theory is worthless. It's not even wrong!

−W. Pauli

To propose a theory, we stipulate a specific design for a theoretical system. Stipulated powers and operations are attributed to the putative system which is idealized, schematic, circumscribed, simplified. It is intended to apply to *kinds* of empirical systems. The relation between the theoretical system and the empirical system is the set-theoretic predicate "is an instance of". A kind of empirical system is, or is not clearly, or is not at all an instance of the idealized theoretical system. When an empirical system does not approximate the definitions of the theoretical system, only the set-theoretic predicate "is an instance of" is considered so inapplicable as to have little epistemic use. The theoretical system, having a range of applications, may still apply to some other empirical system. Being schematic idealizations, theoretical systems cannot be true; they apply or they do not (Colby & Spar, 1983). Every theoretical system has its limits, bounds beyond which it no longer suffices to confer intelligibility−for example, the gas laws do not hold in the interior of the sun.

Not long ago the empirical solar system was thought to be an instance of a (theoretical) Newtonian point-particle system whose "laws" we would now call "definitions." Today we believe that the solar system better approximates the definitions of an Einsteinian point-particle system. An atomic system is not believed to be an instance of an Einsteinian point-particle system, because at this level electromagnetic forces overwhelmingly predominate over gravitational forces, which are taken as negligible.

When optical phenomena did not well approximate the idealized specification of a Newtonian point-particle system, it was not concluded that the system was false but only that light probably did not consist of particles. Copernicus's system succeeded Ptolemy's system, but we still navigate ships and planes with Ptolemy's. A theoretical system is applied depending on the designer's problems, interests, and purposes. The mind was once considered to be an instance of a reflex system; we propose here that aspects of it theoretically approximate a computational system and that this is the right sort of oversimplification to work with.

Mankind has a bad ear for new music.

−Nietzsche

Relations between theories and models can be intricate and esoteric. As mentioned earlier, a theory is a putative set of design specifications for a kind of idealized system, a purely hypothetical, imagined, theoretical object. The designer's specifications describe the structure, the components, and processes of the theoretical object—in our case an algorithmic system. The theory statements consist of sequences of expressions (in natural and/or mathematical language) describing a system assumed to characterize members of a restricted resemblance class that shares specific empirical properties. Models are then constructed as an inquiry procedure for theory clarification and development. Models become tools for critical analysis. Which models are workable and workworthy?

Achinstein (1968) lists five distinguishing characteristics of a theoretical model:

1. It is a set of assumptions about some object or system.
2. These assumptions attribute an inner structure, composition, or mechanism, which manifests itself in other properties exhibited by the object or system.
3. These assumptions are treated as a simplified approximation useful for certain purposes.
4. The model is proposed in the framework of some more basic theory or theories.
5. The model may display an analogy between the object or system described and some other object or system.

In relating theories and models, computational psychology introduces an additional methodologic step: the skilled use of a technical instrument to supplement reflective thinking. This new technologic element results in two sorts of models that are commonly run together in workaday computational discourse. The first, $model_1$, is an abstract model of the theory; the second, $model_2$, the running computer model, involves the technical instrument, a concrete computing system, embodying the abstract $model_1$, whose input/output behavior is empirically observable. In computational psychology, the abstract model attempts to capture the significant structure of the theory in terms of abstract algorithms (well-specified procedures for achieving a desired outcome). How to formulate the abstract procedures of algorithms (superimpositions of abstraction operations) and write out their programs is a challenge for the creative and innovative imagination.

The only true revolt is creation—the revolt against nothingness.

—Ortega y Gasset

Formulating algorithms as theory-types and constructing programs realizing them is difficult because the effort constitutes an inverse problem in contrast to a direct problem. A direct problem, for example, consists of predicting the output from a device given its input and knowledge of its inner mechanisms or finding the value of a function given the function and an input argument. (In $y = f(x)$, compute y given f and x.) An inverse problem consists of designing the mechanisms given only the input/output of a blackbox device or finding the function given its value and the input argument. (Given y and x, find f.) Inverse problems of constructing a system that realizes behavior in a prescribed way, given only the input/output relations, are difficult not only because they require inventiveness but because the designer must grapple with many possible solutions. Input/output behavior patterns can be accounted for by a variety of generating mechanisms. How does one narrow down and constrain the imaginable possible processes to a system that approximates the real processes (Colby, 1977)? For John Locke the essence of an object was "the real constitution of its insensible parts."

At first described in a mixture of natural and technical language accompanied by flow diagrams, an abstract algorithm as theory-type in computational psychology eventually is described in the tokens of a programming language. It is readable (accessible) as a listing of the computer program. The program is run on a computing system, open to public inspection and reproducible by others adept in the techno-logic skills of computational implementation.

Be sure of it: give me the ocular proof.

—Othello

A program is a set of effective procedures for carrying out the interdependent continuities of the computational functions of the algorithm. When the program is run on a computational device, becoming $model_2$, it governs the activity of the physical computing system, whose input/output patterns then replicate the input/output patterns (perceptible simulacra) of the kinds (resemblance classes) in the empirical domain the theory intends to explain. A successful $model_2$ recommends the theory and raises the plausibility of its assumptions. Model$_2$, running under empirical control, is a concrete ostensible object analogous in some respects (it is not a perfect likeness) to the concrete objects (construers) of the resemblance class. Though in loose computationalese talk we sometimes collapse these two models (abstract and running) into one, we must distinguish between them when we consider problems of equivalence and similarity.

In the algorithmic models we are concerned with, the theory and the abstract model (e.g. a flowchart description of the algorithm) are intended to portray as clearly as possible a symboling structure whose functions and subfunctions perform various jobs and communicate their effects to one another. The programmed model actualizes this structure; it is no longer just a description of possible structures. Model$_2$, up and running on a computing system, embodies a structure of symbolic expressions and carries out the effective computational procedures specified in the algorithm. The running model becomes an actual, perceptible member of the restricted resemblance class in the empirical domain. Constructing model$_2$ requires more than clever thinking and argument about the problem; it requires a praxis (hands as well as heads), the use of a skilled technology.

The problems of computational psychology become complicated because the ultimate objects of inquiry are themselves imperceptible semantic-representational models (programs as running processes) in those construers who qualify as members of the resemblance class.

> *To have such a problem, a good problem, is to surmise the presence of something hidden, and yet possibly accessible,* lying in a certain direction.
>
> —Polanyi (italics added)

In meteorology, a mathematical model of a hurricane describes the nonsymbolic *physical* forces a theory postulates to be at work in a purely physical system. A running model$_2$ of the theory does not generate an actual hurricane, nor are its effects experienced by observers as wet. It is not assumed that the hurricane itself is governed by a program. In computational psychology, however, the algorithmic model uses symbols to describe an organization of entities that themselves *are* those symbols a theory postulates to be at work in an algorithm-executing system whose physical tokens have been assigned a coded construal. The processes described in symbols are themselves symbolic. When the algorithm (an abstract procedure) is then implemented and run as a program, the computing system, now *simultaneously* a physicosymbolic system, generates (reproduces) instances of the observable patterns of phenomena in question. It *exhibits* the phenomena, which is more than describing them. Observers interacting with the running model's input/output patterns (the discernible simulacra of the resemblance class) can, using similarity judgments, perceptually experience and measure effects similar to those they experience when interacting with people in the empirical domain of the relevant resemblance class, aspects of whose behavior is postulated to be governed by the underlying structure (a relative invariant) the putative theory describes.

The symbols of the program-instantiated algorithm *represent* the symbols of the real algorithmic systems assumed to underly the behavior of the empirical systems. The physical tokens existing in the real systems (equivalence classes of physical properties) are not identical to the physical tokens of the computing system, but they are vehicles for the same semantic-content construals. The system operates in accordance with these psychosemantic construals. When the computing system of the running model executes the program, we obviously do not take the physical tokens of the hardware/device (switches) transmitting the bestowed meanings as identical to the physical tokens of the brain hardware (groups of neurons).

By way of programs, the abstracta of the theoretical model are embodied in physical tokens, (becoming illata), and hence they are substantial individuals, being causally effective at the physical level of the physicosymbolic system. The posited sameness or likeness is at the level of formal (not physical) equivalence in that the symboling transactions satisfy the same rule specifications operating on the same construals. The symbolic construals of the found-in-nature mental system and the artifactual computing system are assumed to coincide in semantic content inasmuch as similar observable behavior-types are materialized by both. The virtue of a physical computing system is that one can use a purely notational system of symbols, the instruction set of the programmer's manual, to causally influence the device to work in a prescribed way.

Another difference exists between a theoretical model of a hurricane and an algorithmic model of mental systems. To test the hurricane model, observations are conducted on its predictions, for example, that the hurricane will arrive at a certain place at a certain time; the model is not used to generate an actual hurricane. To test a mental algorithmic model, however, one can construct a running model$_2$, a new empirical object, that can produce and replicate the actual phenomena, the significant observable (reportable mental-state) patterns that constitute the properties of the specified reference class. Because the processes at work in the running model are sufficient to reproduce the phenomena, the theory underlying the model correctly (in part and for the time being) describes the symbol-processing operations at work. Tests of the models and of the theories show their shortcomings by helping to eliminate distortions and gross oversimplifications. To take an example from biochemistry, if one has a theory of the structure of insulin and can use it (a praxis) to construct a synthetic insulin with salient properties of natural insulin, the theory is at least correct enough to deserve further attention and further work in the pursuit phase of inquiry.

> *Every thing is what it is, and not another thing.*
>
> —Bishop Joseph Butler

Since no two objects in the world are exactly alike, it is a matter of decision to take (interpret) aspects of two objects as the same or alike. (We assume a concept of similarity implies a concept of difference.) A computational theory postulates that the structure it specifies is similar to an underlying structure of the unknown, real, mental algorithm systems characteristic of (relatively invariant in) actual members of the restricted resemblance class whose mental productions are the phenomena constituting the explananda problems of interest. Only similarity of underlying *structure* is being imputed. This is not to be taken as a material structure but as a functionally homologous organization of computational functions characterizing the superimposition of abstract algorithms. At the semantic- representational level, the symbol-manipulations in the running model are functionally homologous to those in the real mental systems being considered. Although they may differ in detail at the program level, the same algorithms are being executed.

Equivalence has several forms and degrees. A weak (but not negligible) equivalence consists of similarity of output productions only. A stronger, but rough equivalence can be said to exist when the running model$_2$, in response to similar input patterns, produces similar output patterns whose measurable effects are similar to those exhibited by empirical objects of the resemblant reference class. That is, the running model$_2$ makes instances of properties manifest to perceptual pattern-recognition judgments of equivalent observers conversant with the phenomena, who consider the output patterns cogently appropriate and coherent as responses to the input patterns. (See Cummins, 1983, for the distinction between interpretive analysis, in which an outside interpreter takes a system to be of a certain kind, and a characterization in which the system itself understands its own representations.) As is discussed later, members of our deflected resemblance classes manifest similar productions; for example, they produce token expressions of the same semantic type describing mental states. This input/output pattern level of equivalence, though rough, may be good enough for the purposes at hand. It indicates a plausible possibility that the postulated structure might be roughly correct; that is, the theory sufficiently explains the observed phenomena. The inescapable underdetermination of theory by data implies that alternative theories can account for the same observed data-patterns. There are no uniquely correct explanations. Different theories specifying alternative designs may account for the data-patterns.

Manifestly resemblant behavior determining membership in the resemblance class can be produced in different ways by different strategies. The theories are not rivals for the single adequate explanation. Rather, each is adequate to specify a causal path (a set of strategies) leading to the same final productions by members of the reference class. This may eventually result in a further partitioning and refinement of the reference class, a recurring taxonomic problem as knowledge increases (Salmon, 1984, p. 49.)

A stronger equivalence for functional homology would show that the computational steps that the running-process model$_2$ goes through correctly describe the steps gone through (not necessarily in the same order) by the real running processes of the algorithm-executing systems of the resemblance class. Ideally, the components of model$_2$ can be mapped onto the components of the algorithms of reference class construers. In a functional homology, a given function decomposes into subfunctions in roughly the same way. When a relation holds between two components of the running model$_2$—say, between belief and desire in forming the compound entity of an intentional-action plan—a corresponding relation is posited to hold between the homologous counterparts in the real systems (running programs) of the reference class. Strong equivalence implies that the same symbolic semantic contents are undergoing the same symboling transactions according to the procedures specified by the theory. The same algorithm is being carried out inasmuch as the running model$_2$ works according to the same principles as the processes it parallels in actual humans. This sort of functional homology implies that the same semantic-representational jobs are being performed by those procedures specified in the algorithm of the abstract model. Since the same algorithm can be realized by different *programs* in a computational model (for example, they can be written in the programming language of PASCAL or LISP) running on a variety of computing hardwares, the level of comparison for strong functional homology is posited to be at the level of the theory-type of abstract procedures of algorithms, not at the level of individual programs as tokens. What is to be the similarity measure for the "sameness" of algorithms? One suggestion is that two algorithms are strongly equivalent (functionally homologous) when they can be realized by the same program running on a specified computing system (Pylyshyn, 1984). Since genetic differences and individual life histories insure that no two human *programs* are the same in detail, the theoretical quest is to formulate the *algorithmic* equivalences (abstract invariants) of members of the relevant reference class.

13
Deflections

C: A theoretical system stipulates design specifications of a simplified idealized system, with attributed powers and operations, intended to apply to empirical systems of a resemblance class,
a restricted reference class. Deflections from the design specifications
are considered departures from the ideal. Most research efforts
involving a computational theory of mind have been devoted to
capacities we are proud of—solving problems (Newell & Simon,
1972), planning (Sacerdoti, 1977), understanding stories (Dyer, 1983;
Schank & Abelson, 1977). There are other mental capacities and
liabilities we are not so proud of. Yet these departures are worth
attention because they *matter* in human lives—misunderstandings,
misconstruals, inhibited actions, misguided desires, and a variety of
displacements and deflections from the ideal design. Extreme and
enduring negatively valued deflections of mental systems represent
conditions that may activate attempts at correction. Because they
demonstrate striking values of the properties involved, resemblance
classes of the extreme deflections are important for a cognitive science
that needs taxonomically clear cases for computational explanation.

THE IDEAL AND THE EMPIRICAL

Any system, from solar to mental, has a trajectory from birth to death.
A theoretical system designed to apply to empirically identified
systems postulates (as idealizations) that at each stage in its development the system exhibits characteristic capacities and liabilities.
Deflections from these ideals evoke curiosity because they represent

141

departures from our rules of rightness for proper functions assumed for a natural order. Developmental-direction functions or states are postulated as ideals for the life trajectory of the theoretical system. Ideal mental systems have states and processes whose elements can be computationally specified counterparts of intentionalistically de-scribed "beliefs," "desires", and the like. Empirical mental systems approximate the specified ideals to varying degrees. By definition, all empirical mental systems are made up of deflections; they all, in some respect, involve processes that do not fit the idealizations of the theory. The optimal would be the least deflected.

> *When you realize that everybody is a little bit crazy, the*
> *mystery of the world stands explained.*
>
> —M. Twain

The foundational weakness of both psychology and psychiatry is that they lack a reliable taxonomy of classes of empirically identifiable mental systems. What natural kinds of minds are there? This taxo-nomic problem has been virtually ignored by a psychology trying to jump from the status of philosophy to that of advanced physics without doing the pedestrian work of sorting out and grouping natural kinds. Psychiatry has, with abysmal results, tried to form taxonomies based on committee votes (Colby & Spar, 1983). Without a reliable taxonomy, how can psychiatry make reliable diagnoses and evaluate treatments when the groups of patients represent inequivalent populations? Lacking equivalence classes of patients, how can there even be any comparability of research results? Cogni-tive experiments in psychology are performed on subjects often identified only as "undergraduates." The resulting findings have not explained much of anything that matters in the deflections.

How might resemblance classes of mental-system deflections be formed? One way to define a resemblance class is in terms of members who produce similar observable objects (artifacts). Descrip-tions of artifacts, such as linguistic expressions, can serve as the relevant-kind predicates identifying members of the class. In semantic-representational matters, we can stipulate that members of a mental-system resemblance class generate self-descriptive expres-sions (spoken or written sentences) whose tokens are of similar semantic types (Colby & Parkison, 1985). (Dennett, 1982b, has dubbed this approach "heterophenomenology.") In these cases, the empirical invariants (properties common to members of the class) consist of semantic invariants defined by the produced linguistic expressions that are vehicles for expressing the semantics of the underlying self-descriptive construals.

EXTREME DEFLECTIONS

Paranoidness

Some psychiatric patients, as self-describing systems, produce expressions of similar semantic types. For example, people dominated by the paranoid mode characteristicly say things like the following (when the situations are not true):

I am being followed.
The FBI is out to get me.
People talk about me behind my back.
They are watching me.

These are persecutory expressions. They represent false beliefs of being harassed, threatened, harmed, wronged, followed, oppressed, watched, mistreated, vilified. Such beliefs, in the absence of justifying evidence, qualify their possessors for membership in the class "paranoid." The explanatory problem consists of formulating an underlying algorithm, an inner structure of these mental systems making the empirically defined class a taxon whose members share more than empirical properties. They share the abstract invariant of an algorithm as well as the empirical invariants of products of similar semantic type. They behave similarly because they are constructed homologously at the algorithmic (functions and content) level.

Why is paranoidness considered a deflection? Because a conceptual idealization exists that a mental system does not manifest persecutory delusions. Where does that ideal come from? It seems to stem from a social convention embedded in a folk psychology that relies on naive statistical notions of infrequency or on a value judgment that persecutory delusions, being without foundation, are undesirable (socially disruptive?) for a well-functioning mental system.

In medical disorders, health is normal biologic functioning. The elusive norms of medicine are often statistical means with some range of "normal" variation in a population. Normality is an even more elusive concept in mental disorders, which are conceptualized at various levels from the biologic to the semantic representational. In proposing functional homologies between computational and mental systems, we shall limit our considerations to those departures from the ideal that can be characterized at the semantic-representational level. These imperfections or misfittings represent departures from the operations of proper natural (ideal) computational functions.

One deflective property at the semantic-representational level is the capacity for *mis*representing, including a mental system's misrepresenting itself. In the latter case, we are referring not to simple errors but to purposive, goal-pursuing misrepresentation in the interest of self-preserving internal security: self-deception in which the mind plays false with itself, for example pretending it is not pretending in the interest of preserving internal affective well-being (eustasis). This deflection needs explaining by a cognitive science trying to understand mental systems. Reformulated and modified psychoanalytic concepts, systematically combined with additional ideas, might contribute to explanatory theories about a system's purposive misrepresentations of parts of itself.

For example, a programmable theory of the paranoid mode specifies an underlying algorithm, a step-by-step, sequential ordering of processes, as follows. (The algorithm was programmed in the running model known as PARRY, admittedly a crude model but a hint of better things to come [Colby, 1981].) Input from the environment, or from the output of the mental system itself, is semantically interpreted to activate self-defective beliefs organized as patterns in an inference structure. Their activation causes the affect of shame to rise, which leads to an increase in the negative affect of distress. The paranoid strategy for reducing distress is to disavow that one is responsible for any self-defect or inadequacy. Mislocating the source of the trouble, the paranoid mode forms and carries out an action plan whose objective is to blame others for wronging the self. Shame-induced distress is reduced by intentional, goal-satisfying actions toward others, but the self-defective beliefs remain held with a high intensity. The mental system suffers an improper function in credibility assignments, which results in misrepresenting its second-order beliefs, constructing the belief that it is not defective while retaining the first-order belief that it is. This theory represents an explanatory improvement (a) because it accounts for phenomena anomalous for alternative theories (paranoid reactions in cases of false arrest, birth of a deformed child, Wernicke's aphasia, etc.) and (b) because it encompasses, as a special case, a predecessor theory's apparent success in accounting for paranoid modes connected to homosexual feelings (Colby, 1977).

The theory incorporates modified psychoanalytic assumptions

about defense mechanisms whose goals are to protect the system against the inner pain of negative affects. The theory of the paranoid mode specifies shame as the central painful affect and specifies strengths of self-defective beliefs as those representations whose activation leads to a rise in degrees of shame. The algorithm described by the theory is itself not a psychoanalytic formulation, but the conceptual ancestry of some of its components is clear. A running computational model of the theory (PARRY) has successfully passed a number of resemblance tests in which the model is not empirically distinguishable by psychiatric experts from paranoid patients in an initial psychiatric interview (Colby, 1975, 1981). This success does not yet signify that the algorithm is explanatorily adequate but points, however roughly, in that direction. We mention it here as an example of how reformulated psychoanalytic ideas combined with additional concepts can help in developing improved theories and models of the deflections. Another example is a model of neurotic processes (Colby, 1963) whose final version is described in detail in Boden (1987).

Perversions and Provenances

Comprehensive explanation of a system attempts an account of (a) how it works, (b) how it got to be the way it is, and (c) how it undergoes major structural changes over time. Since a computational psychology is interested in the algorithm shared by members of a resemblance class, one naturally asks, "Where did the algorithm come from?"

Methodologic solipsism holds that there can be laws (strict, exceptionless generalizations) only for internal differences among mental states, because we lack a scientific taxonomy of environmental factors that would serve as bound variables in lawful organism-environment relations. If we relax the restriction about strict, exceptionless laws, we can propose organism-environment regularities in the domain of extreme deflections, where historical origins of the conditions represent striking natural experiments that laboratory experiments cannot reproduce. In these cases, the objects and events have no ultimate scientific taxonomy, but they consist of features, properties, patterns, and regularities *salient to the construer* and describable by him in folk-psychologic terms.

S : For years I have struggled with the idea of the provenance of deflections: how does aberrance—the word clinicians use—

come about? At first, it seemed, the definition of aberrance could be taken for granted; but I now know that that comfortable state was the result of accepting myself as the center of the universe. With that comfort gone, plus the belief no one else is that center, I find aberrance more interesting.

For without a fixed point, where is aberrance? The answer could be found in classification, a way of functioning that differentiates without having to rate. That works fine for most areas of study — plants, rocks, chemical elements — but, at least so far, has failed in all efforts to codify mental functions ("affects", "defense mechanisms"), from classifications that try to order those functions to those that try to separate out disease entities (schizophrenia, homosexuality). Perhaps one test of science that psychoanalysis fails is the test of nonjudgmentality. The classifications of the sciences are neutral, not praiseworthy or pejorative: to a biologist a dog is different from, but not better than, a horse. But when studying mental life, we judge our own when we judge others'. We cannot quite separate our inner life from theirs: the observer's desire to be objective is vulnerable. It may also be so in the natural sciences, but scientific method plus an ethos of scepticism protects them from the individual scientist's corruptibility.

Take an area I have studied: erotic perversion (Stoller, 1975b). Despite our efforts, we contaminate the concept with our private morality. "Perversion" has a negative value with implications of stubbornness, rebellion, willful troublemaking, distortion of normality, sinfulness. In recent years, with the impulse toward scientific investigation of perversion, the vocabulary was changed to alleviate pejorative qualities. And so was introduced the neutral term "deviation," which seemed to mean nothing more than a statistical shift from a norm. "Deviation" worked (for a while), since it conjured up an abstract *behavior*, but when one said "the deviant," a *person* was pictured. Then word-magic failed, and "the deviant" found that his deviance was not just statistical. He was still treated like "the pervert". Thus also was the fate for "variation", "variant," and "the variant"; "aberration" and "aberrance." ("The aberrant," as a label for a person, has never caught on. Let the future not bring forth "the deflect" as the next step in sanitizing "perversion".) The present (I hope short-lived) euphemism is "paraphilia." Science triumphant.

What, in erotic life, is not aberrant and who is the reference frame in the universe, the proper judge? Early in the modern study of erotic aberrance, there seemed no problem: aberrance was obvious. If a man could become erotically excited only with a corpse, a shoe, a sheep, or a lock of hair, no problem in criteria arose. The baseline from which measurement of aberrance proceeded was penis-in-vagina, in man and beast. Of course, though my last sentences reflect no problems in definition (as if we were in the presence of universal truth), the description in fact is bound in time and place.

It is the product of a moralistic development of 2,000 years in Western society (which claims the rules are God given). But at other places and at other times, other behaviors were not considered aberrant: It is said, there have been cultures where no word for erotic aberrance/perversion/deviance/variance even existed. Nonetheless, in the statistical sense, many humans (a majority? how large?) many times practice penis-in-vagina. And the Bible, with the institutions that draw instruction from it, excludes from normality all erotic practices except heterosexual genital intercourse. Flirting with declaring them perversions—certainly stating aberrance, (i.e., sin)—this morality condemns as abnormal (a stronger and often preferred word that combines implications of statistics and natural law) everything else, including pre- and extramarital intercourse.

The situation gets even more complicated when we, as psychoanalysts, listen to what people tell us is in their heads. Then we find that even people who practice monogamous, heterosexual intercourse can be filled with daydreams and images as perverse as those of the psychopathology texts. Following those philosophers who know that "if it isn't dirty, it isn't fun," I have suggested that for most people most of the time, a touch of cruelty may be a trace element in erotic fantasy. And cruelty would be on most everyone's aberrance list.

So here we have a definition of normality/aberrance accepted by a majority in principle and in conscience but not in practice. The statistical has disappeared as a criterion for deflection.

We are left then, with a concept of deflection/aberrance/variance/ deviance/paraphilia/perversion from which has been removed a statistical connotation, the replacement being a value judgment: an ideal. In that case, everything is aberrant (which I find both conceptually and in practice an improvement over the present state of discourse on the subject of erotic excitement).

Let me move now to a study that exemplifies Colby's idea that there are natural experiments—extreme and enduring deflections—a cognitive science can use, in place of laboratory experiments, for developing algorithms. The examples, sketched below, are extreme deflections from the norms for masculinity or femininity ("transsexualism") in anatomically normal boys and girls, a deflection easily agreed-on as extreme and enduring. In these conditions, in which biologic males want to become females and females to become males, a set of historical features (provenance) has been isolated. I have suggested that this constellation is causally relevant in producing members of the transsexual resemblance class, having been noted in 15 males and 14 females.

With this illustration we can give cognitive scientists a sense of the usefulness of extreme deflections in creating algorithms and, at the same time, suggest how a psychoanalytic viewpoint, plus immersion in the clinical situation, can contribute to an enriched cognitive science. Let me sketch in the findings (more detailed descriptions are published elsewhere [Stoller, 1968, 1975a, 1975b]) and, at the same time, exemplify how a theory of Freud's can be evaluated by one's mobilizing new observations. I start with Freud's description of the development of masculinity and femininity, first for males, then females.

Given the importance of biologic factors—scarcely dreamed of, much less described, in Freud's lifetime—the boy, says Freud, has two usually insuperable advantages over girls: he starts out heterosexual, since his first love object is a female, his mother; and he has a visible, highly sensual organ, his penis, to embody and signal his maleness. However, despite the at first unabashed intensity of this combination—a male body that expresses his desire for his mother—he is psychologically and biologically far too immature to work out a successful system for gratifying his desires. In addition, Freud says, he senses his father—large, mature, competent—as an overwhelmingly powerful rival. So he must give up hope for his mother and postpone till later years his heterosexual drives. If his mother helps him, without marked trauma and frustration, he is well on his way toward resolving this dangerous conflict. And if father, by his presence, serves as a measure for masculinity and also implies a promise of future heterosexual success, the boy proceeds with his gender and erotic development.

The girl, on the other hand, has, for Freud, essentially insuperable problems that can be only assuaged, not solved (this being the reason why women, Freud believed, are so damaged in character structure). First, the girl starts with a homosexual, not heterosexual, love object, her mother. So she must perform an act of great renunciation in order to move to a heterosexual mode, that is, to desire her father. Second, she, with (as Freud saw it) an inadequate genital—out of sight and erotically immature as well as incompetent—must spend her development chronically disappointed and envious. Her chances of negotiating these perils are poor. (How strange these sentences and those to come must seem to the nonclinically experienced cognitive scientist.)

My version of gender development differs from Freud's in two ways, one inconsequential, the other significant. The inconsequential difference is that I have available the biologic and behavioristic research done since Freud's time. So I can better describe—precisely at times—how these factors work in development and (great comfort!) can refer to them knowing they are not simply speculations in a philosophic discourse. The consequential factor is my noting a stage in gender development—core gender identity—that begins at birth and therefore precedes the period when Freud's description begins. In my* version, the first stage of gender development is spent with the infant (male or female) sometimes more, sometimes less merged physically and psychologically with mother, the infant only gradually becoming aware of a separation. This merging is powerfully reinforced by biologic necessity, neoteny that produces an infant unable to survive birth without mother's presence. This presence is not only a life-and-death necessity for the infant but also, to the extent that it approaches perfection, the ultimate happiness—bliss; absence of pain, distress, frustration, terror. There are, of course, biologic factors (e.g., neuromuscular development) that push an infant toward separating from mother's body and psyche. (In lower animals, these are more marked in males than females; I suspect that is so in humans as well.) But if something should interfere with the natural unfolding of separation—if the infant, male or female, is too close, too long, too blissfully—then the infant's sensing himself or herself as a creature separate from mother is delayed. Should that happen with a girl, whatever the price in the development of independence and competence, merging with mother's body and psyche ("identification") favors femininity. Unfortunately, the same holds for the boy: He too may become feminine, if this influence is strongly present.

Because the pull to mother is so enticing, so gratifying, a boy must create inside himself a dam against this interior pull toward merging with her. This barrier—this set of beliefs, desires, counterdesires, opinions about oneself and others—I have called "symbiosis anxiety" or "merging anxiety." It takes the form of fantasies (though I believe its underpinning is biologically and behavioristically reinforced) that tell the boy he does not want to be a female, to be like a female, or to be too close to females lest their femaleness and femininity pull him

---

*"My" connotes squatter's more than discoverer's rights, for others have, in one way or another, disagreed with Freud's description.

back to that earliest, blissful, protofeminine state. Much of what is defined as masculinity is, I believe, the manifestation of this hidden process.

Girls, on the other hand, need not create the same barrier to symbiosis. Though they must do something of the same sort in order to become separate beings, society's demands—reinforcements—do not push them to avoid femininity. I therefore conclude, contrary to Freud, that women are not naturally more wretched than men.

The resultant rules, confirmable by observations (Stoller, 1968, 1975a, 1985) but needing much more testing are as follows:

1. If a boy is held too intimately, with too little frustration, with too much pleasure, and too long against his mother's body *and* psyche, he is at risk for maldeveloping his masculinity.
2. The risk increases when his father is not sufficiently present to shield the son against the mother's influence and is not present as a model for masculinity.
3. When, in the case of a girl, the mother-infant symbiosis is disrupted (the opposite effect to that in these feminine boys), the child risks becoming masculine.
4. The risk increases the more her father moves in and is intrusively present.
5. The stronger these factors, the greater the gender reversal.
6. Given these dynamics in the family, marked femininity will occur in a boy and marked masculinity in a girl. But the hypotheses do not say that *all* feminine boys and *all* masculine girls emerge from such dynamics. Our two examples—the most feminine of biologically intact males and the most masculine of biologically intact females—test the rules. In the origins of . certain cases in both sexes, the mother–infant symbiosis is a powerful factor. When extremely feminine boys are studied in childhood, I find in many of my cases that there is a family pattern in which the mother has transsexual desires (that is, in childhood, she said, quite literally, that she hoped to grow a penis), the father distant or absent, the boy beautiful and graceful, and the mother–infant son relationship extremely close (Stoller, 1968, 1975a, 1985). These mothers try to maintain indefinitely a blissfully intimate symbiosis with their son, he being chosen over his mother's other children because she perceived him from birth on to be physically beautiful, cuddly, and loving. And in these cases, father is an absent nonentity.

The reverse dominates the situation with extremely masculine girls, where mother was unable (perhaps because sorely depressed) to function adequately as a mother during this daughter's infancy, the baby having been perceived by the mother as not pretty, not feminine, not cuddly. And the girl's father moves into the vacuum caused by mother's inability to mother, with father being the close parent. Unfortunately, father and daughter join not in a heterosexual style but with father encouraging his daughter to be like him.

Let me summarize this summary. Freud states (and, for several generations after, psychoanalysts—though with a few dissenters—believe they have confirmed in their treatment of patients) that males and masculinity are superior to females and femininity. This is because boys have the more natural (unimpeded) development: maleness is biologiclly superior to, and masculinity more dependable, effective, and stable than, femininity. An anchor for Freud's argument is that the boy begins life with a heterosexual love object, his mother.

I, however, in studying certain extremely deviant children—markedly feminine males and markedly masculine females—and their families find a different story. Missing from Freud's account but intensely present in the life history of the males I studied is a first stage, through which all infants must pass: a merging with mother, during which she is not distinguished as a separate person, a love object. Only gradually—and with these feminine boys terribly discouraged by mother—is merging transformed into separation and individuation from mother, with the result that a boy is encouraged to be male and masculine.

Freud, despite leaving it out of his description of the development of masculinity and femininity, always emphasized this early, blissful stage of merging. And, though the description of it has been much improved by direct infant observation, none of the observers claim that the infant springs from the womb with a full-blown sense of identity. All boys not bereft of mothers, therefore, must try to negotiate this passage from not distinguishing themselves from their mothers (a protofemininity) to knowing that they are males who should be masculine. My hypothesis states that the mothers who try to prevent that separation and individuation put their sons at risk for femininity.

We have, then, a "natural experiment" in which a major hypothesis of Freud's is tested in the clinic by means of the aberrant case.

Semantic Structural Change

The universe is transformation; our life is what our thoughts make it.

—Marcus Aurelius

The past is a foreign country; they do things differently there.

—L.P. Hartley

How do I know: What can I hope? What should I do?

—Kant

C: Computational psychology has not devoted much attention to the problem of semantic structural change in human adulthood. Not only do human mental systems grow from birth and evolve, they are subject to change throughout their life trajectory. Beliefs acquired from past experience, especially in childhood and adolescence, become idle and no longer contribute to intentionalistic action. New implicational rules are added. Introspective self-awareness increases (Churchland, 1984). Desires are abandoned as unrealizable. Simplistically rigid control rules of childhood ("Don't be selfish") are made conditional and liberal to become appropriate to adult circumstances. Self-specifications as to one's own nature undergo transformations.

The current psychotherapies using semantic inputs provide a crude technology for intervention in attempting to modify semantic structures and the behavior they direct. This psychoeducational technology, based on rules-of-thumb and common sense psychology, has little scientific underpinning. It relies on capacities of cognitive penetratability and self-reprogramming. The question is no longer whether psychotherapies are effective (some are on some people) but why and how they work when they do. What causal, control, and self-corrective processes are involved? How can this rough technology for the relief of mental suffering be improved through systematic cognitive inquiry, particularly in cases of unwanted extreme deflections? In a spirit of interfield rapproachment, we have suggested that there are a few ideas from psychoanalytic theory that can contribute to computational psychology. In addition, we suggest the latter might also contribute to the traditional domain of psychoanalysis, psychodynamic psychotherapy, by the development of expert systems, as is currently done in artificial intelligence (Colby et al. 1987). At the end, it looks like a two-way street.

14

Conclusions

C & S: We have argued that cognitive science is a promising new approach to a science of aspects of mind that can be symbolically represented. The approach involves theory specification and computational model building designed to explain the regularities in the phenomena shared by members of equivalence classes. We believe some psychoanalytic ideas (such as unconscious processes and defensive strategies) can be usefully incorporated in computational theories and models.

We conclude that psychoanalysis can contribute to a science of the mind when it is no longer the psychoanalysis we know but flows into a more effective science and technology: cognitive science. And, we believe, cognitive science in its present fledgling condition also will not grow into a science of the mind until it confronts the important problems of real minds, such as the fantasies and feelings of real people. We do not know how it will happen; our book is not intended to specify the how. We can only describe the why and then, exercising the prerogative of tribal elders, pass the task along to the next generation.

We are suggesting, in ways others have not, that the work can be done. First, psychoanalysts can get rid of their bad habits: too few facts, too much rhetoric, and self-deceiving proclamations of being a science.

Second, psychoanalysts might take on, enjoy, and reward the role of naturalist: discoverer and describer, in ordinary language, of the contents of equivalence classes of minds, what they are, and how they came to be.

Third, attempts at a science of mind should turn to the cognitive sciences with a computational theory of mind as well as a powerful new instrument, the computing system.

Fourth, cognitive science should have a go at the challenge of modeling such mental processes as consciousness, multiple consciousnesses ("homunculi"), self-deception, desire, fantasy, person-to-person misunderstanding, and the inhibition of intentional action.

Fifth, cognitive science might systematically improve the currently crude psychoeducational technologies designed to change semantic-representational structures in the extreme deflections.

This done, Adam and Eve will have taken a large bite of the apple.

References

Abelson, R. P. (1963). Computer simulation of 'hot' cognition. In S. Tomkins & S. Messick (Eds.), *Computer Simulation of Personality*. New York: Wiley.

Abelson, R. P. (1973). The structure of belief systems. In R. C. Schank & K. M. Colby (Eds.), *Computer Models of Thought and Language*. San Francisco: Freeman.

Abelson, R. P. (1981). Constraint, construal, and cognitive science. *Third Annual Conference of the Cognitive Science Society*, pp. 1–9.

Achinstein, P. C. (1968). *Concepts of Science: A Philosophical Analysis*. Baltimore: Johns Hopkins University Press.

Balter, L., Lothane, Z., & Spencer, J. H. (1980). On the analyzing instrument. *Psychoanalytic Quarterly*, 49:474–504.

Barclay, J. R. (1964). Franz Brentano and Sigmund Freud. *Journal of Existentialism*, 17:1–36.

Barron, S., & Tuchman, M. (1980). *The Avant-Garde in Russia 1910-1930: New Perspectives*. Los Angeles County Museum of Art.

Baudry, F. D. (1982). A silent partner to our practice: The analyst's character and attitude. *Association for Psychoanalytic Medicine Bulletin*, 21:110–118.

Bechtel, W. (1983). A bridge between cognitive science and neuroscience: the functional architecture of the mind. *Philosophical Studies*, 44:319–330.

Bechtel, W. (1985). Realism, instrumentalism, and the intentional stance. *Cognitive Science*, 9:473–497.

Black, M. (1979). More about metaphors. In A. Ortony (Ed.), *Metaphor and Thought*. Cambridge: Cambridge University Press.

Boden, M. (1977). *Artificial Intelligence and Natural Man*, 2nd ed. New York: Basic Books, 1987.

Bohm, D. (1980). *Wholeness and the Implicate Order*. London: Ark.

Boorstin, D. J. (1983). *The Discoverers*. New York: Random House.

Braginski, V. B., Vorontsov, Y. I., & Thorne, K. S. (1980). Quantum nondemolition measurements. *Science*, 209:547–558.

Brand, M. (1984). *Intending and acting*. Cambridge, MA: MIT Press.

Breger, L. (1981). *Freud's Unfinished Journey*. London: Routledge & Kegan Paul.

Brenner, C. (1968). Psychoanalysis and science. *Journal of the American Psychoanalytic Association*, 16:675–696.

Brenner, C. (1980). Metapsychology and psychoanalytic theory. *Psychoanalytic Quarterly*, 49:189–214.

Bunge, M. (1983). *Treatise on Basic Philosophy. Epistemology and Methodology II. Understanding the World,* Dordrecht: D. Reidel.

Chessick, R. D. (1980). The problematical self in Kant and Kohut. *Psychoanalytic Quarterly,* 49:456–473.

Chiland, C. (1980). Clinical practice, theory and their relationship in regard to female sexuality. *International Journal of Psycho-analysis,* 61:359–365.

Churchland, P. (1984). *Matter and Consciousness.* Cambridge, MA: MIT Press.

Clippinger, J. H. (1977). *Meaning and Discourse: A Computer Model of Psychoanalytic Speech and Cognition.* Baltimore: Johns Hopkins University Press.

Cohen, I. B. (1985). *Revolution in Science,* Cambridge, MA: Harvard University Press.

Colby, K. M. (1963). Computer simulation of a neurotic process. In S. Tomkins & S. Messick (Eds.), *Computer Simulation of Personality.* New York: Wiley. (This program is described in detail in Boden, 1977.)

Colby, K. M. (1973). Simulation of belief systems. In R. C. Schank & K. M. Colby (Eds.). *Computer Models of Thought and Language.* San Francisco: Freeman.

Colby, K. M. (1975). *Artificial Paranoia: A Computer Simulation of Paranoid Processes,* New York: Pergamon Press.

Colby, K. M. (1977). An appraisal of four psychological theories of paranoid phenomena. *Journal of Abnormal Psychology,* 86:54–59.

Colby, K. M. (1978). Mind models: An overview of current work. *Mathematical Biosciences,* 39:159–185.

Colby, K. M. (1981). Modeling a paranoid mind. *Behavioral and Brain Sciences,* 4:515–560.

Colby, K. M. (1986). Ethics of computer-assisted psychotherapy. *Psychiatric Annals,* 16:414–415.

Colby, K. M., & Spar, J. E. (1983). *The Fundamental Crisis in Psychiatry: Unreliability of Diagnosis,* Springfield, IL. Charles C. Thomas.

Colby, K. M., & Parkison, R. C. (1985). Linguistic conceptual patterns and key-idea profiles as a new kind of property for a taxonomy of neurotic patients. *Computers and Human Behavior,* 1:181–194.

Colby, K. M., Gould, R., Aronson, G. & Colby, P. M. (1987). Computer psychotherapy programs as expert systems. A model of common-sense reasoning underlying intentional nonaction and its use in remediation of stress-related conditions. (Under review).

Collins, S. (1980). Freud and "the riddle of suggestion." *International Review of Psycho-Analysis,* 7:429–437.

Crews, F. (1986). Beyond Sulloway's Freud: Psychoanalysis minus the myth of the hero. In *Skeptical Engagements.* New York: Oxford University Press.

Culler, J. (1975). *Structuralist Poetics.* Ithaca, NY: Cornell University Press.

Cummins, R. (1983). *The Nature of Psychological Explanation,* Cambridge, MA: Bradford/MIT Press.

Dahl, H. (1974). The measurement of meaning in psychoanalysis by computer analysis of verbal contexts. *Journal of the American Psychoanalytic Association,* 22:37–57.

Dahl, H., Teller, V., Moss, D., & Trujillo, M. (1978). Countertransference examples of the syntactic expression of warded-off contents. *Psychoanalytic Quarterly,* 47:339–363.

Decker, H. S. (1977). *Freud in Germany. Psychological Issues,* Monogr. 41. New York: International Universities Press.

Dennett, D. C. (1969). *Content and Consciousness,* London: Routledge and Kegan Paul.

Dennett, D. C. (1978). *Brainstorms: Philosophical Essays on Mind and Psychology,* Cambridge, MA: Bradford/MIT Press.

Dennett, D. C. (1981). Three kinds of intentional psychology. In R. Healey (Ed.),

Reduction, Time, and Reality. Cambridge: Cambridge University Press.

Dennett, D. C. (1982a). Beyond belief. In A. Woodfield (Ed.), *Thought and Object.* Oxford: Clarendon Press.

Dennett, D. C. (1982b). How to study consciousness empirically or nothing comes to mind. *Synthese,* 53:159–180.

Dennett, D. C. (1987). *The intentional stance.* Cambridge, MA: Bradford/MIT Press.

Devereux, G. (1967). *From Anxiety to Method in the Behavioral Sciences.* The Hague: Mouton.

Dretske, F. (1981). *Knowledge and the Flow of Information.* Cambridge, MA: MIT Press.

Dyer, M. G. (1983). The role of affect in narratives. *Cognitive Science,* 7:211–242.

Edelson, M. (1977). Psychoanalysis as science. *Journal of Nervous and Mental Disease,* 165:1–28.

Edsall, J. T. (1981). Two aspects of scientific responsibility. *Science,* 212:11–14.

Einstein, A., & Infeld, L. (1938). *The Evolution of Physics.* New York: Simon & Schuster.

Ellenberger, H. F. (1970). *The Discovery of the Unconscious: the History and Evolution of Dynamic Psychology.* New York: Basic Books.

Ellman, S. J., & Moskowitz, M. B. (1980). An examination of some recent criticisms of psychoanalytic "metapsychology." *Psychoanalytic Quarterly,* 49:631–662.

Erdelyi, M. H. (1985). *Psychoanalysis. Freud's Cognitive Psychology.* New York: W. H. Freeman.

Ericcson, K. A., & Simon, H. A. (1984). *Protocol Analysis: Verbal Reports as Data.* Cambridge: Bradford/MIT Press.

Esman, A. H. (1979). On evidence and inference or the Babel of tongues. *Psychoanalytic Quarterly,* 48:628–630.

Farrell, B. A. (1981). *The Standing of Psychoanalysis.* New York: Oxford University Press.

Fodor, J. A. (1975). *The Language of Thought.* New York: Crowell.

Fodor, J. A. (1980). Methodological solipsism considered as a research methodology in cognitive psychology. *Behavioral and Brain Sciences,* 3:63–209.

Fodor, J. A. (1981). *Representations: Philosophical Essays on Mind and Psychology.* Cambridge, MA: MIT Press.

Fodor, J. A. (1983). *The Modularity of Mind: An Essay on Faculty Psychology.* Cambridge, MA: Bradford/MIT Press.

Fodor, J. A. (1987). *Psychosemantics: The Problem of Meaning in the Philosophy of Mind.* Cambridge, MA: Bradford/MIT Press.

Freud, S. (1905). Three essays on the theory of sexuality. *Standard Edition,* 7:130–245. London: Hogarth, 1953.

Freud, S. (1905). Jokes and their relation to the unconscious. *Standard Edition,* 8. London: Hogarth Press, 1960.

Freud, S. (1913). The claims of psycho-analysis to scientific interest. *Standard Edition,* 13:165–190. London: Hogarth Press, 1955.

Freud, S. (1914). On narcissism: An introduction. *Standard Edition,* 14:73–102. London: Hogarth Press, 1957.

Freud, S. (1915). Instincts and their vicissitudes. *Standard Edition,* 14:117–140. London: Hogarth Press, 1957.

Freud, S. (1917). Introductory lectures on psychoanalysis. *Standard Edition,* 15 & 16. London: Hogarth Press, 1963.

Freud, S. (1918). Lines of advance in psychoanalytic therapy. *Standard Edition,* 17:159–168. London: Hogarth Press, 1955.

Freud, S. (1924). On the history of the psychoanalytic movement. *Standard Edition,* 14: London: Hogarth Press, 1966.

Freud, S. (1925). An autobiographical study. *Standard Edition,* 20:7–74. London: Hogarth Press, 1959.

Freud, S. (1933a). Anxiety and instinctual life. *Standard Edition*, 22:81–111. London: Hogarth Press, 1964.

Freud, S. (1933b). The question of a *weltanschauung*. *Standard Edition*, 22:158–182. London: Hogarth Press, 1964.

Freud, S. (1937). Constructions in analysis. *Standard Edition*, 23:255–269. London: Hogarth Press, 1964.

Freud, S. (1938). An outline of psychoanalysis. *Standard Edition*, 23:144–207. London: Hogarth Press, 1964.

Freud, S. (1940). The psychical apparatus and the external world. *Standard Edition*, 23:144–147. London: Hogarth Press, 1964.

Gill, M. M., & Brenman, M. (1947). Problems in clinical research. *American Journal of Orthopsychiatry*, 17:196–230.

Gill, M. M., & Hoffman, I. Z. (1982). *Analysis of Transference. Vol. II. Studies of Nine Audio-recorded Psychoanalytic Sessions*. New York: International Universities Press.

Gill, M. M., Simon, J., Fink, G., Endicott, N. A., & Paul, I. H. (1968). Studies in audio-recorded psychoanalysis: I. general considerations. *Journal of the American Psychoanalytic Association*, 16:230–244.

Glover, E. (1952). Research methods in psycho-analysis. *International Journal of Psycho-analysis*, 33:403–409.

Grünbaum, A. (1983). The foundations of psychoanalysis. In L. Laudan (Ed.), *Mind and Medicine: Problems of Explanation and Evaluation in Psychiatry and the Medical Sciences*. Berkeley: University of California Press.

Grünbaum, A. (1984). *The Foundations of Psychoanalysis: a Philosophical Critique*. Berkeley: University of California Press.

Grünbaum, A. (1986). Precis of *The Foundations of Psychoanalysis: a Philosophical Critique*. (Peer commentary and author's response). *Behavioral and Brain Sciences*, 9:217–284.

Guntrip, H. (1978). Psychoanalysis and some scientific and philosophical critics. *British Journal of Medical Psychology*, 51:207–224.

Harrison, S. I. (1970). Is psychoanalysis "our science"? Reflections on the scientific status of psychoanalysis. *Journal of the American Psychoanalytic Association*, 18:125–149.

Hartmann, H. (1958). Comments on the scientific aspects of psychoanalysis. In *Essays on Ego Psychology*. New York: International Universities Press, 1964.

Harty, M. K. (1986). Action language in the psychological test report. *Bulletin of the Menninger Clinic*, 50:456–463.

Haugeland, J. (1985). *Artificial Intelligence: The Very Idea*. Cambridge, MA: Bradford/MIT Press.

Heisenberg, W. (1958). *Physics and Philosophy*. New York: Harper & Row.

Holland, J. H., Holyoak, K. J., Nisbett, R. E., & Thagard, P. R. (1986). *Induction: Processes of Inference, Learning, and Discovery*. Cambridge, MA: MIT Press.

Holt, R. R. (1961). Clinical judgment as a disciplined inquiry. *Journal of Nervous and Mental Disease*, 133:369–382.

Holt, R. R. (1981). The death and transfiguration of metapsychology. *International Review of Psycho-Analysis*, 8:129–143.

Hook, S. (Ed.) (1959). *Psychoanalysis, Scientific Method, and Philosophy: A Symposium*. New York: New York University Press.

Jacobsen, P. B., & Steele, R. S. (1979). From present to past: Freudian archeology. *International Review of Psycho-Analysis*, 6:349–362.

James, W. (1980). *Principles of Psychology*. Vol I. New York: Dover.

Jones, E. (1953). *The Life and Work of Sigmund Freud, Vol 2*. New York: Basic Books.

Joseph, E. D. (1975). Psychoanalysis—science and research: Twin studies as a paradigm. *Journal of the American Psychoanalytic Association*, 23:3–31.

Kaplan, A. H. (1981). From discovery to validation: A basic challenge to psychoanalysis. *Journal of the American Psychoanalytic Association*, 29:3–26.

Kennedy, G. (1959). Protoscience and metapsychology. In S. Hook (Ed.), *Psychoanalysis, Scientific Method, and Philosophy: A Symposium*. New York: New York University Press.

Kernberg, O. F. (1986). Institutional problems of psychoanalytic education. *Journal of the American Psychoanalytic Association*, 34:799–834.

Kitcher, P. (1985). Narrow taxonomy and wide functionalism. *Philosophy of Science*, 52:78–97.

Klein, M. I. (1981). Freud's seduction theory. *Bulletin of the Menninger Clinic*, 45:185–208.

Knapp, P. H. (1974). Segmentation and structure in psychoanalysis. *Journal of the American Psychoanalytic Association*, 22:14–36.

Kohut, H. (1970). Scientific activities of the American Psychoanalytic Association. *Journal of the American Psychoanalytic Association*, 18:462–484.

Kohut, H. (1983). Introspection, empathy, and the semicircle of mental health. *International Journal of Psycho-Analysis*, 63:395–405.

Kris, E. (1952). *Psychoanalytic Explorations in Art*. New York: International Universities Press.

La Barre, W. (1980). Personality from a psychoanalytic viewpoint. In *Culture in Context*. Durham, NC: Duke University Press.

Laplace, P. S. (1820). *A Philosophical Essay on Probabilities*. New York: Dover, 1951.

Laudan, L. (Ed.) (1983). Mind and medicine. Berkeley: University of California Press.

Leibniz, G. W. (1714). The monadology. In G. R. Montgomery (Trans.), *Leibniz*. LaSalle, IL: Open Court, 1902.

Leites, N. (1971). *The New Ego*. New York: Science House.

Lem, S. (1978). *A Perfect Vacuum*. New York: Harcourt Brace Jovanovich.

Levine, F. J. (1980). Responses to Dr. Paul Tolpin. *Journal of the Philadelphia Association for Psychoanalysis*, 7:13–20.

Lustman, S. L. (1963). Some issues in contemporary psychoanalytic research. The *Psychoanalytic Study of the Child*, 18:51–74. New York: International Universities Press.

Lycan, W. G. (1981). Toward a homuncular theory of believing. *Cognition and Brain Theory*, 4:139–159.

Lycan, W. G. (1987). *Consciousness*. Cambridge, MA: Bradford/MIT Press.

Mahony, P. J. (1986). *Freud and the Rat Man*. New Haven: Yale University Press.

Marras, A. (1985). The Churchlands on methodological solipsism and computational psychology. *Philosophy of Science*, 52:295–309.

Maxwell, J. C. (1868). (From a letter quoted in A. Pais.) *Subtle is the Lord: The Science and Life of Albert Einstein*. New York: Clarendon, 1982.

McCarthy, J. (1960). Programs with common sense. *Proceedings of the Symposium on Mechanization of Thought Processes*. London: Her Majesty's Stationery Office.

McIntosh, D. (1979). The empirical bearing of psychoanalytic theory. *International Journal of Psychoanalysis*, 60:405–431.

Medawar, P. B. (1969). *Induction and Intuition in Scientific Thought*, Philadelphia: American Philosophy Society.

Medawar, P. B. (1975). Victims of psychiatry. *New York Review of Books*, January 23.

Merlan, P. (1945). Brentano and Freud. *Journal of the History of Ideas*, 6:375–377.

Merlan, P. (1949). Brentano and Freud—a sequel. *Journal of the History of Ideas*, 10:375–377.

Minsky, M. (1963). Steps toward artificial intelligence. In E. A. Feigenbaum & J. Feldman (Eds.), *Computers and Thought*. New York: McGraw-Hill.

Minsky, M. (1986). *The Society of Mind*. New York: Simon & Schuster.

Modell, A. H. (1978). Affects and the complementarity of biologic and historical meaning. *Annual of Psychoanalysis* 6:167–180. New York: International Universities Press.

Mueller, E. T. (1987). *Daydreaming and Computation: A Computational Theory of Everyday Creativity, Learning, and Emotions in the Human Stream of Thought.* Unpublished doctoral dissertation, Department of Computer Science, University of California at Los Angeles.

Nagel, E. (1959). Methodological issues in psychoanalytic theory. In S. Hook (Ed.), *Psychoanalysis, Scientific Method, and Philosophy: A Symposium.* New York: New York University Press.

Nelson, R. J. (1982). *The Logic of Mind,* Dordrecht: D. Reidel.

Newell, A. (1973). Artificial intelligence and the concept of mind. In R. C. Schank & K. M. Colby (Eds.), *Computer Models of Thought and Language.* San Francisco: Freeman.

Newell, A. (1981). Physical symbol systems. In D. A. Norman (Ed.), *Perspectives on Cognitive Science,* Norwood, NJ: Ablex.

Newell, A. (1982). The knowledge level. *Artificial Intelligence,* 18:87–127.

Newell, A., & Simon, H. A. (1972). *Human Problem Solving.* Englewood Cliffs, NJ: Prentice-Hall.

Peterfreund, E. (1983). *The Process of Psychoanalytic Therapy.* Hillsdale, NJ: The Analytic Press.

Peterfreund, E. (1986). The heuristic approach to psychoanalytic therapy. In J. Reppen (Ed.), *Analysts at Work.* Hillsdale, NJ: The Analytic Press.

Pollock, G. H. (1980). Freud as scientist and psychoanalysis as science. *The Annual of Psychoanalysis,* 8. New York: International Universities Press.

Popper, K. R. (1971). *The Open Society and its Enemies, Vol. II.* New York: Harcourt, Brace & World.

Popper, K. R. (1974). Replies to my critics. In P. A. Schilpp (Ed.), *The Philosophy of Karl Popper.* La Salle, IL: Open Court.

Putnam, H. (1975). *Mind, Language, and Reality: Philosophical papers. Vol. II.* Cambridge: Cambridge University Press.

Pylyshyn, Z. (1983). Representation, computation, and cognition. In F. Machlup & U. Mansfield (Eds.), *The Study of Information.* New York: Wiley.

Pylyshyn, Z. (1984). *Computation and Cognition: Toward a Foundation of Cognitive Science.* Cambridge, MA: Bradford/MIT Press.

Reik, T. (1933). New ways in psycho-analytic technique. *International Journal of Psycho-Analysis,* 14:321–334.

Ricoeur, P. (1974). Structure and hermeneutics. In D. I. Ihde (Ed.), *The Conflict of Interpretations: Essays in Hermeneutics.* Evanston, IL: Northwestern University Press.

Riviere, J. (1958). A character trait of Freud's. In J. D. Sutherland (Ed.), *Psychoanalysis and Contemporary Thought.* London: Hogarth Press.

Rothstein, R. (1980). The scar of Sigmund Freud. *New York Review of Books,* October 9.

Roustang, F. (1982). *Dire Mastery.* Baltimore: Johns Hopkins University Press.

Rubinstein, B. B. (1980). The problem of confirmation in clinical psychoanalysis. *Journal of the American Psychoanalytic Association,* 28:397–417.

Sacerdoti, E. D. (1977). *A Structure for Plans and Behavior.* New York: Elsevier.

Salmon, W. C. (1984). *Scientific Explanation and the Causal Structure of the World.* Princeton, NJ: Princeton University Press.

Saw, R. L. (1954). *Leibniz.* London: Penguin.

Schank, R. C., & Abelson, R. P. (1977). *Scripts, Plans, Goals and Understanding.* Hillsdale, NJ: Lawrence Erlbaum Associates.

Schank, R. C., & Colby, K. M. (1973). *Computer Models of Thought and Language.* San Francisco: Freeman.

Schwaber, P. (1976). Scientific art: The interpretation of dreams. *The Psychoanalytic Study of the Child*, 31:515–533. New York: International Universities Press.

Schrödinger, E. (1951). *Science and Humanism*. Cambridge: Cambridge University Press.

Seitz, F. D. (1966). The consensus problem in psychoanalytic research. In L. A. Gottschalk & A. H. Auerbach (Eds.), *Methods of Research in Psychotherapy*. New York: Appleton-Century-Crofts.

Selfridge, O. G. (1958). Pandemonium: A paradigm for learning. In L. Uhr (Ed.), *Pattern Recognition*. New York: Wiley.

Sellars, W. (1963). *Science, Perception and Reality*. London: Routledge & Kegan Paul.

Shakow, D. (1960). The recorded psychoanalytic interview as an objective approach to research in psychoanalysis. *Psychoanalytic Quarterly*, 29:82–97.

Silverman, L. H., & Wolitzky, D. L. (1981). Toward the resolution of controversial issues in psychoanalytic treatment. In S. Slipp (Ed.), *Curative Factors in Dynamic Psychotherapy*. New York: McGraw-Hill.

Simon, H. A. (1969). *The Sciences of the Artificial*. 2nd Ed. Cambridge, MA: MIT Press, 1981.

Simon, H. A. (1981). Cognitive science: The newest science of the artificial. In D. A. Norman (Ed.), *Perspectives on Cognitive Science*. Norwood, NJ: Ablex.

Slap, J. W., & Levine, F. J. (1978). On hybrid concepts in psychoanalysis. *Psychoanalytic Quarterly*, 47:499–523.

Spence, D. P. (1981). Psychoanalytic competence. *International Journal of Psycho-Analysis*, 62:113–124.

Steele, R. S. (1979). Psychoanalysis and hermeneutics. *International Review of Psycho-Analysis*, 6:389–411.

Steele, R. S., & Jacobsen, P. B. (1978). From present to past: the development of Freudian theory. *International Review of Psycho-Analysis*, 5:393–422.

Stich, S. (1983). *From Folk Psychology to Cognitive Science: The Case Against Belief*. Cambridge, MA: MIT Press.

Stoller, R. J. (1968). *Sex and Gender, Vol. I*. New York: Science House.

Stoller, R. J. (1975a). *Sex and Gender, Vol. II*. London: Hogarth.

Stoller, R. J. (1975b). *Perversion*. New York: Pantheon.

Stoller, R. J. (1985). *Presentations of Gender*. New Haven: Yale University Press.

Stoller, R. J., & Geertsma, R. H. (1963). The consistency of psychiatrists' clinical judgements. *Journal of Nervous and Mental Disease*, 137:58–66.

Stone, L. (1981). Madness. *New York Review of Books*. December 16.

Sulloway, F. J. (1979). *Freud, Biologist of the Mind: Beyond the Psychoanalytic Legend*. New York: Basic Books.

Toulmin, S. (1957). *The Philosophy of Science*. London: Hutchinson.

Waelder, R. (1962). Psychoanalysis, scientific method, and philosophy. *Journal of the American Psychoanalytic Association*, 10:617–637.

Wallerstein, R. S. (1986). Psychoanalysis as a science: A response to new challenges. *Psychoanalytic Quarterly*, 55:414–451.

Wallerstein, R. S. (1976). Psychoanalysis as a science. In M. M. McGill & D. S. Holzman (Eds.), *Psychology versus Metapsychology: Psychoanalytic Essays in Memory of George S. Klein*, (pp. 198–228). New York: International Universities Press.

Wallerstein, R. S., & Sampson, H. (1971). Issues in research in the psychoanalytic process. *International Journal of Psycho-Analysis*, 52:11–50.

Webster's Third New International Dictionary (1961). Springfield, IL: Merriam.

Whyte, L. L. (1960). *The Unconscious Before Freud*. New York: Basic Books.

Will, D. (1980). Psychoanalysis as a human science. *British Journal of Medical Psychology*, 53:201–211.

Wimsatt, W. C. (1972). Teleology and the logical structure of function statements.

Studies in the History and Philosophy of Science, 3:1–80.

Wimsatt, W. C. (1980). Reductionist research strategies and their biases in the units of selections controversy. In T. Nickles (Ed.), *Scientific Discovery, Vol. 2: Case Studies.* Dordrecht: D. Reidel.

Ziman, J. (1978). *Reliable Knowledge: An Exploration of the Grounds For Belief in Science.* Cambridge: Cambridge University Press.

Zimmerman, D. (1983). Relationships among training analysts. *Annual of Psychoanalysis,* 11:99–122.

Zukav, G. (1980). *The Dancing Wu Li Masters.* New York: Bantam.

AUTHOR INDEX

SUBJECT INDEX

A

Aberrance, 145–147
Affect, 130, 144
Algorithm, 18–24, 119, 134, 138
  as theory-type, 135
Analogy, 15–16, 18–21
Artificial intelligence, 12, 13, 14, 129–130
Autonomous psychology, 21–24

B

Behaviorism, 5, 129
Belief, 111, 112, 113, 120, 129, 142, 143, 149, 152
Brentano's problem, 19

C

Cargo Cult science, 28
Cartesian cut, 16
Cause, 17, 19–20, 23, 137
Chess-playing programs, 130–131
Class
  reference, 23, 120, 137
  resemblance, 21, 135, 139
Clinical evidence, 29, 31
Cognitive engineering, 130–131
Cognitive inquiry, 1, 9–14, 152
Cognitive penetrability, 13, 24, 152
Cognitive science, 1, 5–6, 14, 26, 33, 38, 39, 89, 109, 112–113, 130, 131, 141, 148, 153–154

Common sense psychology, 109–113, 130
Computational
  analogy, 5, 15, 122
  explanation, 131, 132
  functions, 120–122
  model, 2, 13, 22, 113, 120, 121, 130, 131, 153
  psychology, 13, 22, 33, 122, 129, 131, 152
  theory of mind, 17, 18, 27, 110, 130, 141
Computer science, 129
Computing system, 14, 15, 16, 19, 130, 135
Connectionism, 15
Conscious, 27
Consensibility, 9, 82, 132
Consensual validation, 82–83
Consensus, 9, 79–80, 82
Construal, 13, 17, 23, 110, 136–137, 143
Countertransference, 87

D

Data, 3, 11–12, 26, 29–32, 41–75, 131, 139
Default rules, 23
Defense mechanisms, 33, 36, 144–145
Deflections, 24, 26, 33, 34, 113, 141–152
Delusion, 143
Description, 29